BOBBY DEEN'S
EVERYDAY
EATS

BOBBY DEEN'S
EVERYDAY EATS

BOBBY DEEN

BALLANTINE BOOKS TRADE PAPERBACKS 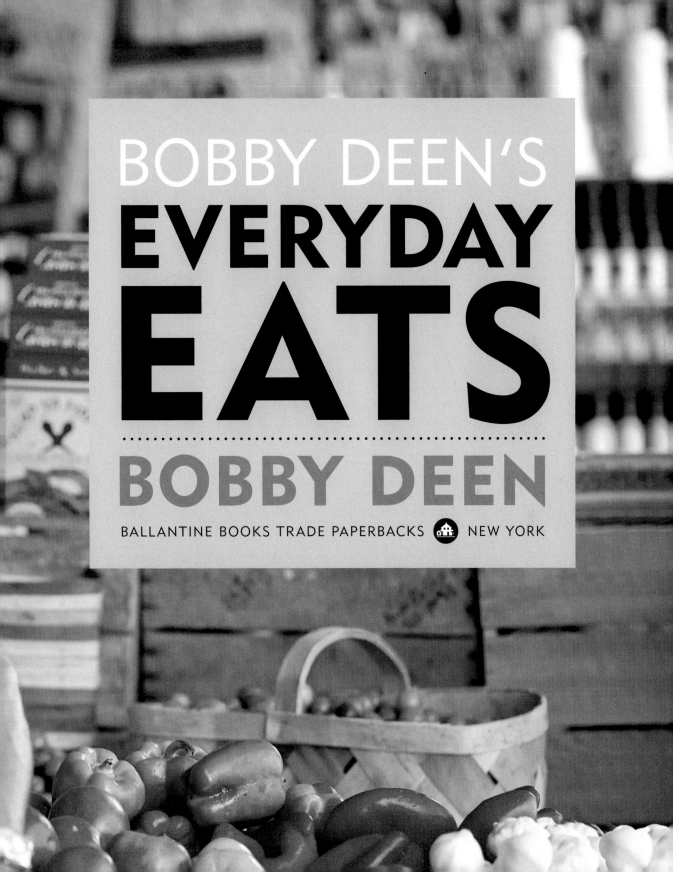 NEW YORK

A Ballantine Books Trade Paperback Original

Copyright © 2014 by Bobby Deen Enterprises LLC

Published in the United States by Ballantine Books, an imprint of
Random House, a division of Random House LLC,
a Penguin Random House Company, New York.

BALLANTINE and the HOUSE colophon are registered trademarks
of Random House LLC.

Photography by Ben Fink Photography

ISBN 978-0-8041-7716-0
eBook ISBN 978-0-8041-7717-7

Printed in the United States of America on acid-free paper

www.ballantinebooks.com

9 8 7 6 5 4 3 2 1

Book design by Liz Cosgrove

This book is dedicated to my beautiful new bride.
Claudia, you make every day that much more wonderful.
I feel so blessed to be sharing my life with you.
I just know it's going to be an amazing journey.

CONTENTS

4 POULTRY

5 MEAT

6 MEATLESS MAINS

7 FIRE UP THE GRILL

8 SEASONAL SIDES

9 GOOD FOR YOU GRAINS

10 SWEET DREAMS

INTRODUCTION

WE ALL HAVE THAT ONE WELL-LOVED COOKBOOK that's dog-eared and generously splattered with who-knows-how-many food stains. It's the one that gets us through dinner prep most nights of the week. Well, you might want to move that one to the side to make room for this one. You're going to want to keep this cookbook at the ready because these pages contain pretty much everything you'll need for fast, delicious, healthy weeknight eating throughout the year.

Let's face it: Our schedules are overstuffed. Unfortunately, far too often our bellies are as well. Somehow, getting dinner on the table quickly has become synonymous with unhealthy eating. I say it's time to break that connection. We may not be able to de-clutter our busy lives, but we sure do have the power to dial down the fat and calories we're eating—as long as the alternative is just as easy and delicious.

Who among us doesn't love a home-cooked meal? I'm talking fresh, filling, satisfying food made by you or someone you love. Now that I'm a married man, it's so nice to have someone to share my weeknight meals with at home. Claudia and I trade off who does the cooking and who does the washing up. Suddenly I find myself looking forward to weeknight dinners like never before.

A tasty weeknight meal for me these days might mean quick comfort foods such as **PASTA WITH BEEF BOLOGNESE** (page 94) or **SHRIMP AND RICE** (page 44). Or it might feature a new and exciting dish I've learned about through traveling around the country and meeting up with fellow food personalities. New entrées in my repertoire include Jamaican-style **QUICK JERK CHICKEN** (page 67) and dishes with less common ingredients such as tofu. The first time I tried marinated tofu, I couldn't believe how tasty it was. It gave me the idea to create **BAKED BBQ TOFU** (page 118), a dish that highlights how wonderful this protein-packed ingredient is when you layer it with a full-flavored sauce. It's a perfect entrée for a Meatless Monday.

I think it's fair to say that when it comes to food, I want it all. Apart from fast, easy, and healthy, it also has to be delicious and decadent tasting. If I can't fit indulgent dishes on my menu such as **PORK CUBANO SANDWICHES** (page 98) and **RASPBERRY MOUSSE** (page 192), it just won't work out for me. If I'm going to eat right, it simply can't feel like deprivation. In recipes like these, I sub out the more fat- and calorie-laden ingredients and find healthier alternatives. In the Cubano, I use lean tenderloin instead of fatty pork shoulder, and in my velvety mousse I turn to light whipped topping as opposed to heavy cream.

To stock up for dinners throughout the week, I do my food shopping over the weekend. I make sure the kitchen is filled with good, fresh ingredients Claudia and I both love, and with healthy pantry staples that are the building blocks for simple yet great-tasting meals. With fresh fish and produce in the house, I can put together a satisfying main course salad like **ROASTED SALMON AND CHERRY TOMATO SALAD** (page 17). And using pantry staples, I can create a meal around **HEARTY VEGETARIAN BURGERS** (page 117). To help you stock up wisely, be sure to check out the Stocking Up section in Pantry Ideas (page 195) at the end of this book. It contains a handy guide to the items you'll need to construct a healthy pantry, fridge, and freezer.

Each recipe in this book has fewer than 350 calories and can be prepared in less than thirty minutes. This emphasis on speedy home cooking is really great for the body. I find that having the right ingredients in the house and easy recipes at my fingertips makes me more likely to cook something myself rather than stop for takeout on the way home. And because being prepared is the key, I've designed a set of daily menus for you to use throughout the week, as well as descriptions of semi-homemade meals that can be pulled together in mere minutes. These under-1,500-calorie menus and instant pantry meals can be found following the recipe chapters at the end of this book.

It seems that more and more people are finding ways to make their lifestyle a healthier one. Why, I've seen it happen in my own family. When Mama, Michael, and Jamie started getting fit and dropping weight, I knew things were really changing. Collectively, we've lost over 180 pounds in the last few years. That's a whole person! I've also been lucky to have as my best friend a man who set me on that path over ten years ago. Sam Carter helped it all click into place for me back then when he told me, "I can't guarantee you *quantity* of life, but if you stick with the exercise, I can guarantee you *quality* of life." Those are words to live by.

I invest time in the gym, so why wouldn't I pay close attention to what I eat? Because I work so hard on the physical side, I don't want to blow it all on the food I put in my body. The meals you'll find in this book consist of the staples of any healthy diet—fresh fruits and vegetables, lean meats, and whole grains. You can get all the ingredients at any supermarket. The recipes contain no tricks, just good straightforward techniques that make cooking after a long day of work a no-fuss affair. In the end, it comes down to this: If you keep it simple and load up your meals with great flavor, maintaining a balanced diet will start to feel like no big deal. Until the results start to show. Then, just as I did, you'll realize just how big a deal this healthy eating thing really is, in the most awesome way.

BOBBY DEEN'S
EVERYDAY
EATS

I AM A BIG SALAD EATER. And by that I mean, I like 'em on the larger side. I can't tell you how many weeknights I get home from work and find myself craving a hearty salad for dinner. Sometimes I like my salad on the side, but more often than not, I fix one that's satisfying enough to serve as my main meal. That means adding some favorite proteins and healthy starches to help fill me up.

I don't eat salads just because they're good for me. I choose to eat them because they are delicious and the options are limitless. First off, there's the endless array of salad greens out there on the supermarket shelves. I can choose earthy spinach one day, spicy arugula the next, and crunchy romaine on the third day to keep things interesting. I dress the leaves up with all sorts of goodies: meats, cheeses, fish, veggies, you name it. Take my **NIÇOISE SALAD** (page 14), for instance. It's got tuna, olives, and potatoes all nestled among peppery baby arugula leaves. Now if that isn't a meal, I don't know what is.

Salads are also a great way of putting your leftovers to good use. And for midweek eating, that sure is handy. I tend to cook a lot over the weekend and stock up my refrigerator with bits and pieces for the week. Dinner prep for a main course salad can consist of quickly foraging through the fridge for ingredients and tossing them all together in a big bowl. That's how I came up with my **ROAST CHICKEN AND BREAD SALAD** (page 20). With leftover rotisserie chicken in the fridge and a half-used loaf of bread on the countertop, inspiration struck. Forget about dinner in less than thirty minutes. Try dinner in less than fifteen minutes!

While each of the salads in this chapter can be paired with bottled dressings, I've included a homemade dressing recipe with each. I didn't always make my own dressings. I'd go out to a restaurant, order a salad as my entrée, and feel really good about my choice. But then I realized that the heavy dressings that you find on most restaurant menus are actually packed with fat and calories. Now I tend to stick with my homemade concoctions and the occasional light bottled dressing. It's made a world of difference.

Salads are a great place to be creative. Even if you are a totally novice cook, you can feel pretty safe about experimenting when it comes to salads. So use these recipes as a jumping-off point to create your own masterpiece. And let your imagination go a little wild. Your body will thank you for it.

HOPPIN' JOHN SALAD

This pretty Southern salad is a great place to use any kind of leftover rice. I love meals that make good use of leftovers—they help me be less wasteful and give me a leg up on getting my dinner together quickly. This salad is fresh and zingy and makes for a nice accompaniment to easy grilled fish or chicken. Or for a thoroughly Southern style meal, serve this dish with my *Bourbon-Braised Pork Chops* (page 99). **SERVES 6**

1 can (15½ ounces) black-eyed peas, rinsed and drained

1½ cups cooked brown or white rice

1 cup chopped yellow bell pepper

1 cup grape tomatoes (about ¼ pound), halved

2 scallions, white and light green parts only, chopped

1 tablespoon olive oil

1 tablespoon fresh orange juice

2 teaspoons red wine vinegar

Pinch of Cajun spice blend

Salt and freshly ground black pepper

1 In a large bowl, toss together the black-eyed peas, rice, bell pepper, tomatoes, and scallions.

2 In a small bowl, whisk together the oil, orange juice, vinegar, Cajun spice blend, and salt and pepper to taste. Pour over the pea and rice mixture, and toss to combine.

Nutritional count based on 6 servings (does not include salt and black pepper to taste): 148 calories, 3g protein, 3g fat, 28g carbohydrate, 3g fiber, 126mg sodium

HEARTY THREE-BEAN SALAD

This hearty three-bean salad relies on both red wine vinegar and sherry vinegar for a one-two punch of flavor. Rounded out with fresh parsley and basil, this protein-packed dish is herby, tangy, and super satisfying. **SERVES 6**

1 shallot, thinly sliced

1 garlic clove, finely chopped

3 tablespoons red wine vinegar

2 tablespoons sherry vinegar

½ teaspoon salt

3 tablespoons olive oil

1 can (15½ ounces) cannellini beans, rinsed and drained

1 can (15½ ounces) chickpeas, rinsed and drained

1 can (15½ ounces) red kidney beans, rinsed and drained

1 teaspoon freshly ground black pepper

1 tablespoon finely chopped fresh parsley

1 tablespoon finely chopped fresh basil

Baby salad greens, for serving

In a large bowl, combine the shallot, garlic, red wine vinegar, sherry vinegar, and salt. Whisk in the oil. Add the cannellini beans, chickpeas, and kidney beans, and season with the pepper. Stir to combine, then sprinkle with the parsley and basil. Serve over the baby greens.

LET IT SIT: This is one of those awesome salads that gets better with time. Minus the salad greens, it will keep, covered, in the fridge for about 3 days. I like to make this in the morning before I leave the house for the day so that it's all set to serve when I come home at night.

Nutritional count based on 6 servings (does not include salad greens for serving): 248 calories, 9g protein, 8g fat, 33g carbohydrate, 8g fiber, 538mg sodium

DEVILED EGG SALAD

I love a get-together that features deviled eggs on the appetizer lineup. They're one of my favorite party foods. Since I can't be at a party every day of the week, I've found a way to enjoy the taste of the classic deviled egg by deconstructing it into this clever little salad meal. The dressing features the traditional tangy flavor and creamy texture of the original dish, while the crunchy lettuce, radishes, and bacon bring the meal to new heights by adding texture and color. **SERVES 4 / MAKES ⅔ CUP DRESSING**

DRESSING

¼ cup light mayonnaise
¼ cup light sour cream
1 tablespoon Dijon mustard
½ teaspoon hot sauce
½ teaspoon Worcestershire sauce
Juice of ½ lemon
2 tablespoons olive oil
Pinch of salt
Freshly ground black pepper

SALAD

9 large eggs
1 head romaine lettuce (about 1 pound),
    torn into bite-size pieces
5 radishes, thinly sliced
3 strips turkey bacon, cooked and crumbled
4 scallions, white and light green parts only,
    thinly sliced

1 To make the dressing: In a medium bowl, whisk together the mayonnaise, sour cream, mustard, hot sauce, Worcestershire, lemon juice, oil, salt, and 1 tablespoon of water. Season to taste with black pepper.

2 To prepare the salad: In a medium saucepan, cover the eggs by 1 inch with cold water. Bring to a boil over medium heat. Remove from the heat and let sit, covered, for 9 minutes. Meanwhile, fill a medium bowl with ice water. When the eggs are done, drain them, transfer to the ice water, and let sit for 5 minutes, or until cool. Peel the eggs and halve them crosswise. Pop the yolks out and discard them (or reserve them for another use), and then cut the halves into ¼-inch-thick slices.

3 Divide the lettuce, radishes, and sliced egg whites evenly among four plates. Drizzle with the dressing and garnish with the bacon, scallions, and more black pepper if you like. Serve immediately.

NO YOKE: While I discard the yolks in this recipe, you should feel free to keep them in the mix if you really like them. Just be aware that you'll be adding a fair bit of fat and calories into the dish. Or if you like, compromise: Keep half the yolks and discard the rest.

Nutritional count based on 4 servings (does not include black pepper to taste):
202 calories, 12g protein, 15g fat, 7g carbohydrate, 2g fiber, 518mg sodium

FRENCH BISTRO SALAD

My wife, Claudia, really loves this salad, so when it's date night, it's a pretty good bet I'll be in the kitchen putting this dish together. Don't get too hung up on the fancy lettuce the recipe calls for. It works well with any type of green you might have on hand, or even a mix of a few different types. What really makes this salad special is the smoky, bacon-y warm vinaigrette that coats the delicate lettuce leaves. If you enjoy a runny yolk, do as I do and give the poached egg a tap with your fork as you sit down to eat. The yolk will break over your salad and mingle with the vinaigrette, delivering a burst of deep flavor to the greens. **SERVES 4**

3 strips turkey bacon, thinly sliced crosswise
2 tablespoons red wine vinegar
1 teaspoon Dijon mustard
2 tablespoons olive oil
¼ teaspoon salt
½ teaspoon freshly ground black pepper,
   plus more for serving
1 tablespoon distilled white vinegar
8 cups frisée, curly endive, or baby spinach
4 large eggs
Snipped fresh chives, for serving

1 In a deep, medium nonstick skillet over medium heat, cook the bacon until it is beginning to crisp, about 8 minutes. Using a slotted spoon, transfer the bacon to a paper-towel-lined plate to drain. Remove the skillet from the heat and, stirring constantly, add the red wine vinegar, mustard, and oil. Immediately pour the vinaigrette into a small heat-proof bowl and season with the salt and pepper. Clean out the skillet with a paper towel so you can cook the eggs in it.

2 Fill the cleaned-out skillet with 2 inches of water, add the white vinegar, and bring to a boil over high heat.

3 Meanwhile, evenly distribute the frisée, curly endive, or baby spinach among four individual plates.

4 When the water in the skillet comes to a boil, reduce the heat to a gentle simmer. Break one of the eggs into a small cup and then slide the egg into the water, stirring the water very gently with a spoon. Repeat immediately with the other eggs, and cook until the whites are firm, about 3 minutes. Remove the eggs with a slotted spoon and drain them on paper towels.

5 Transfer one egg to each bed of greens, and drizzle with the warm vinaigrette. Garnish with the bacon, black pepper to taste, and the snipped chives, and serve.

Nutritional count based on 4 servings (does not include black pepper or chives for serving): 232 calories, 14g protein, 18g fat, 5g carbohydrate, 3g fiber, 732mg sodium

SHRIMP TACO SALAD

This salad has pretty much everything I love in a meal. It's got plump and juicy shrimp paired up with velvety Boston lettuce, creamy avocado, crunchy, spicy red radishes, and fiesta-worthy Southwest flavors. When I feel like splurging a little, I add some low-fat Cheddar cheese to the mix and spoon a dollop of Greek yogurt right there on top. It doesn't get much better than this, folks. **SERVES 4**

1 pound medium shrimp, peeled and deveined

1½ teaspoons olive oil

1 teaspoon chili powder

1 teaspoon ground cumin

Pinch of cayenne pepper

Juice of 1 lime

1 teaspoon honey

½ teaspoon salt

3 small (4-inch diameter) corn tortillas

1 large head Boston lettuce (about ¾ pound), cored and chopped

1 large avocado, pitted, peeled, and chopped

5 radishes, thinly sliced

½ small red onion, thinly sliced

¼ cup chopped fresh cilantro

Jarred salsa, for serving

Lime wedges, for serving

1 Preheat the oven to 400°F.

2 In a medium bowl, combine the shrimp, 1 teaspoon of the oil, chili powder, cumin, cayenne, lime juice, honey, and ¼ teaspoon of the salt. Cover and let the shrimp marinate in the fridge while you prepare the tortillas.

3 Stack the tortillas on top of each other, slice them in half, and then slice them crosswise into thin strips. In a bowl, toss the tortilla strips with the remaining ½ teaspoon oil and the remaining ¼ teaspoon salt. Spread them on a rimmed baking sheet, and bake until they are crisp and beginning to brown, about 12 minutes. Halfway through the tortilla baking time, scrape the shrimp onto another rimmed baking sheet and add it to the oven. Bake the shrimp until opaque, about 8 minutes.

4 Evenly divide the lettuce, avocado, radishes, red onion, and shrimp among four plates. Sprinkle the baked tortilla strips and chopped cilantro over each plate. Serve with the salsa and lime wedges.

NO COOK: You can make this dish even easier by buying precooked shrimp and baked tortilla chips from the supermarket. Add flavor to the shrimp by tossing it in the marinade and letting it sit for about 15 minutes or so. I like this option on a hot summer day when I just can't think about turning on my oven.

Nutritional count based on 4 servings (does not include salsa and lime for serving):
265 calories, 26g protein, 10g fat, 20g carbohydrate, 5g fiber, 213mg sodium

GRILLED STEAK SALAD

This simple summer salad gets most of its fantastic flavor from the smoke of the barbecue. It doesn't take much to transform quality fresh ingredients like flank steak, romaine lettuce, tomato, and avocado into something really special. Grilling the lemon brings a sweet caramelized flavor to the juice that is squeezed on top. **SERVES 4**

½ pound flank steak

¼ teaspoon salt, plus more to taste

½ teaspoon freshly ground black pepper, plus more to taste

3 teaspoons olive oil

1 large red onion, cut into 8 wedges

1 lemon, halved

1 large head romaine lettuce (about 1½ pounds), halved lengthwise through the root

½ pint cherry tomatoes, halved

1 medium avocado (about 5 ounces), pitted, peeled, and chopped

¼ cup grated Parmesan cheese

Chopped fresh basil, for serving

1 Lightly grease a grill grate with cooking spray, and preheat the grill to high heat.

2 Rub the flank steak all over with the salt, pepper, and 1½ teaspoons of the oil.

3 In a small bowl, toss the onion with ½ teaspoon of the oil. When the grill is hot, add the lemon, cut sides down. Grill the lemon, without flipping it, until charred and lightly caramelized, about 4 minutes. Transfer the lemon to a cutting board and put the onion and flank steak on the grill. Grill the onion, covered, until charred and tender, about 4 minutes per side. Grill the flank steak, covered, for 3 to 5 minutes per side, or until the internal temperature reaches 130°F for medium-rare or a few minutes longer for medium, depending on what you prefer. Transfer the onion and steak to the cutting board with the lemon, loosely cover the steak and onion with foil, and let rest for 5 minutes.

4 Meanwhile, grill the lettuce halves, cut side down, for 1 minute, or until lightly charred but still green and crisp. Transfer to a cutting board.

5 Roughly chop the grilled lettuce and distribute it among four individual serving plates. Thinly slice the flank steak against the grain. Scatter the tomatoes, avocado, onion, and steak slices over the lettuce. Lightly squeeze the lemon halves over the salads, and drizzle each salad with the remaining 1 teaspoon oil. Sprinkle with the Parmesan and more salt and pepper to taste, and garnish with the chopped basil.

Nutritional count based on 4 servings (does not include basil for serving and salt and black pepper to taste):
245 calories, 17g protein, 15g fat, 12g carbohydrate, 5g fiber, 303mg sodium

NIÇOISE SALAD

A classic Niçoise salad can contain as many as 600 calories per serving. My version has half that amount. The creamy yogurt-based dressing I created was instrumental in lightening things up. It's no secret that I'm absolutely crazy for yogurt. I eat it on its own, I make dressings and marinades out of it, and I replace the cream in my desserts with it. I find it so versatile. **SERVES 6**

8 small red potatoes (about ½ pound), unpeeled, halved

2 tablespoons red wine vinegar

2 teaspoons Dijon mustard

1 teaspoon honey

2 tablespoons olive oil

2 tablespoons low-fat plain yogurt

¼ teaspoon salt, plus more to taste

½ teaspoon freshly ground black pepper, plus more for serving

3 cups green beans (about ½ pound), trimmed

4 cups packed baby arugula

2 vine-ripened tomatoes (about ¾ pound), cut into wedges

2 cans (5 ounces each) tuna packed in water, drained

¼ cup pitted kalamata olives

1 In a medium pot, cover the potatoes with cold salted water. Bring to a boil over medium-high heat and cook until the potatoes are tender, about 15 minutes.

2 Meanwhile, in a medium bowl, combine the vinegar, mustard, honey, oil, yogurt, salt, and pepper.

3 With the potato water continuing to boil, use a slotted spoon to transfer the cooked potatoes to the bowl of vinaigrette. Toss to coat thoroughly in the vinaigrette.

4 Fill a medium bowl with ice water. In the same pot of boiling water used to cook the potatoes, cook the green beans for 1½ minutes. Drain in a colander and then immediately transfer to the ice water. Drain the cooled beans and pat dry with a paper towel.

5 On four individual plates, or on one large platter, evenly distribute the arugula. Arranging each ingredient in bunches, add the tomatoes, tuna, olives, and cooked potatoes and green beans. Drizzle the remaining vinaigrette over the salad. Serve garnished with more black pepper.

Nutritional count based on 6 servings (does not include black pepper for serving): 300 calories, 20g protein, 6g fat, 43g carbohydrate, 6g fiber, 363mg sodium

ROASTED SALMON AND CHERRY TOMATO SALAD

It doesn't take much to toss this meal together, and yet it looks beautiful on the plate. So when I've got unexpected midweek guests, I serve this salmon. My friends always think I've gone to a whole lot of trouble to make them feel welcome. In reality, this dish gets me in and out of the kitchen super fast, allowing me to spend more time with my guests. I like to serve *Brown Rice with Peas and Parmesan* (page 174) on the side. **SERVES 4**

4 skinless salmon fillets (5 ounces each)

1 teaspoon salt

1¾ teaspoons freshly ground black pepper

3 teaspoons plus 1 tablespoon olive oil

3 cups cherry tomatoes (about 1½ pounds), halved

2 teaspoons finely chopped fresh basil

2 teaspoons balsamic vinegar

4 cups baby arugula

2 teaspoons fresh lemon juice

1 Preheat the oven to 400°F.

2 Season the salmon fillets with ½ teaspoon of the salt and 1 teaspoon of the pepper, and drizzle with 2 teaspoons of the oil.

3 In a large bowl, toss the cherry tomatoes with 1 teaspoon of the oil, ¼ teaspoon of the salt, and ¼ teaspoon of the pepper. Spread the tomatoes on a rimmed baking sheet, and add the salmon fillets to the same baking sheet.

4 Roast until the fish is flaky and almost cooked through and the tomatoes are tender, 12 to 15 minutes. Remove from the oven and transfer the salmon to a plate.

Cover it loosely with aluminum foil and let it rest for 10 minutes. Transfer the tomatoes to a medium bowl, and toss with the basil and ¼ teaspoon pepper.

5 In a large bowl, whisk together the vinegar, remaining ¼ teaspoon salt, and remaining ¼ teaspoon pepper until combined. Whisk in the remaining 1 tablespoon oil. Add the arugula and toss until it is coated. Add the roasted tomatoes and toss gently to combine. Top the arugula salad with the roasted salmon, and drizzle with the lemon juice. Serve immediately.

SUMMER LUNCH: This dish tastes great at room temperature as well. That's how I like to serve it when I have company over for lunch. If I'm serving it room temperature, I dress the arugula salad just as my guests are sitting down to eat. That way the greens don't wilt under the vinaigrette.

Nutritional count based on 4 servings: 338 calories, 32g protein, 19g fat, 9g carbohydrate, 3g fiber, 663mg sodium

SNOW PEA SALAD WITH PEANUT CHICKEN

Slicing the chicken before you bake it not only makes it cook in a flash, it also gives you more peanut flavor in each and every bite. Be sure you boil the snow peas just until they turn bright green and then give them a rinse under cold water after you drain them from the hot water. That way they will stay nice and crisp, the perfect contrast to the tender, juicy chicken. **SERVES 4**

¼ cup crunchy or smooth peanut butter

1 tablespoon plus 1 teaspoon vegetable oil

3 teaspoons fresh lime juice

2½ teaspoons low-sodium soy sauce

2 teaspoons red wine vinegar

1 teaspoon dark brown sugar

¼ teaspoon chili powder

⅛ teaspoon ground ginger

1 small garlic clove, finely chopped

1 pound boneless, skinless chicken breast halves, cut crosswise into ¾-inch-thick slices

¾ pound snow peas, trimmed

1 teaspoon toasted sesame oil

1 Preheat the oven to 450°F. Grease a rimmed baking sheet with cooking spray.

2 In a medium bowl, combine the peanut butter, the 1 tablespoon vegetable oil, 2 teaspoons of the lime juice, 2 teaspoons of the soy sauce, the vinegar, brown sugar, chili powder, ginger, and garlic, and stir until smooth. Add the chicken and toss until evenly coated. Transfer to the prepared baking sheet and bake until the chicken is cooked through, 8 to 10 minutes.

3 Meanwhile, bring a medium pot of salted water to a boil over high heat. Add the snow peas and cook for 1 minute, until crisp-tender. Drain in a colander, run under cold water to cool down, and drain well again. Transfer to a medium bowl.

4 In a small bowl, whisk together the sesame oil, remaining 1 teaspoon vegetable oil, remaining 1 teaspoon lime juice, and remaining ½ teaspoon soy sauce. Add to the snow peas and toss until evenly coated. Divide among four plates and top with the chicken.

Nutritional count based on 4 servings: 290 calories, 31g protein, 13g fat, 11g carbohydrate, 3g fiber, 246mg sodium

BUFFALO CHICKEN SALAD

Sticky, sweet, and spicy Buffalo chicken wings are one of my favorite indulgences when I've got my buddies over to watch the big game on Sunday. For games during the week, however, I like to re-create those flavors in a lighter, but equally satisfying, salad. This dish features all the great taste of the bar food classic: sweet and spicy red sauce, creamy blue cheese, and crunchy celery. The only things missing are the extra fat and calories. **SERVES 6 / MAKES 1 CUP DRESSING**

CHICKEN

1 tablespoon plus 1 teaspoon olive oil

1½ tablespoons hot sauce

½ teaspoon sweet paprika

2 teaspoons ketchup

½ teaspoon salt

1½ pounds chicken tenders

DRESSING

⅓ cup crumbled blue cheese

½ cup light sour cream

1 tablespoon light mayonnaise

1 tablespoon fresh lemon juice,
   plus more to taste

½ tablespoon white wine vinegar

Dash of Worcestershire sauce

¼ teaspoon hot sauce

¼ teaspoon salt, plus more to taste

Freshly ground black pepper to taste

SALAD

1 large head romaine lettuce,
   torn into bite-size pieces

3 celery stalks, finely chopped

½ cup light green celery leaves, for garnish

Freshly ground black pepper to taste

1 To prepare the chicken: In a medium bowl, combine the oil, hot sauce, paprika, ketchup, and salt. Add the chicken and toss to coat. Let the chicken marinate at room temperature while the oven is preheating.

2 Preheat the oven to 375°F.

3 Place the chicken tenders on a rimmed baking sheet and bake for 12 to 15 minutes, until cooked through.

4 Meanwhile, make the dressing: In a medium bowl, combine the blue cheese, sour cream, mayonnaise, lemon juice, vinegar, Worcestershire, hot sauce, salt, and 1 tablespoon of water. Add more water if you want to thin it out more, and adjust the seasonings with salt and pepper to taste.

5 Assemble the salad: Divide the lettuce, chopped celery, chicken, and dressing evenly among six plates. Serve garnished with the celery leaves and black pepper.

Nutritional count based on 6 servings (does not include celery leaves for garnish and salt and black pepper to taste):
285 calories, 33g protein, 15g fat, 5g carbohydrate, 1g fiber, 620mg sodium

ROAST CHICKEN AND BREAD SALAD

I typically make this salad on nights when I've got leftover rotisserie chicken—one of my favorite convenience foods—in the fridge. About half a chicken provides the perfect amount for this dish. **SERVES 4 / MAKES ⅔ CUP VINAIGRETTE**

SALAD

½ small whole-wheat baguette (about 7 inches), cut into 1-inch cubes

½ rotisserie chicken, skin and obvious fat removed, meat cut into 1-inch cubes (about 1½ cups)

1 seedless English cucumber (about 10 ounces), cut into ½-inch cubes

3 small vine-ripened tomatoes (about ¾ pound), chopped

½ small red onion, thinly sliced

¼ cup pitted kalamata olives, thinly sliced

½ cup chopped fresh parsley

Freshly ground black pepper to taste

VINAIGRETTE

3 tablespoons white wine vinegar

½ tablespoon Dijon mustard

1 teaspoon honey

1 teaspoon dried oregano

¼ teaspoon salt

½ teaspoon freshly ground black pepper

¼ cup olive oil

1. **To make the salad:** Position an oven rack about 10 inches from the heat and preheat the broiler to low.

2. On a rimmed baking sheet, place the bread cubes in a single layer. Toast under the broiler for 3 minutes, or until crisp and beginning to brown. Watch them carefully so they don't burn.

3. **Meanwhile, make the vinaigrette:** In a small bowl, combine the vinegar, mustard, honey, oregano, salt, and pepper. Whisk in the oil until combined.

4. In a large bowl, combine the bread cubes, chicken, cucumber, tomatoes, onion, and olives. Add just enough vinaigrette to coat. Mix in the parsley, and season with black pepper if you think it needs it.

Nutritional count based on 4 servings (does not include black pepper to taste): 349 calories, 18g protein, 19g fat, 28g carbohydrate, 3g fiber, 477mg sodium

CHICKPEA SALAD WITH PITA CROUTONS

Salads like this one are why God made hot summer days. With cool mint and cucumber in the mix, I challenge you to find a more refreshing salad for the dog days of July and August. I don't eat this salad only on blazing hot days, though. I whip this salad up whenever I need to remind myself that summer is a-coming, even if the thermometer outside is saying something else. This salad is the perfect accompaniment to just about any of the grilled meats in chapter 7, but I especially love to serve it with the *Buttermilk and Herb–Marinated Grilled Chicken Thighs* (page 131). **SERVES 6**

3 whole-wheat pitas (6½-inch diameter)

1½ teaspoons olive oil

Salt to taste

1 teaspoon cumin seeds

1 cup low-fat Greek yogurt

½ cup coarsely chopped fresh mint

2 cans (15½ ounces each) chickpeas, rinsed and drained

2 cucumbers (6 ounces each), peeled, seeded, and chopped

2 tomatoes (6 ounces each), cored and chopped

2 garlic cloves: one cut in half, the other finely chopped

Freshly ground black pepper to taste

1 Preheat the oven to 400°F.

2 Brush the pitas with the oil and season with salt to taste. Place on a rimmed baking sheet and bake until crisp, 5 to 7 minutes.

3 Meanwhile, heat a small skillet over medium heat. Add the cumin seeds and toast for 1 minute, until lightly colored and aromatic. Transfer the cumin to a medium bowl and stir in the yogurt and mint. Add the chickpeas, cucumbers, tomatoes, chopped garlic, and salt and pepper to taste, and stir to combine.

4 Rub each baked pita with a cut end of the halved garlic clove, and cut each pita into 8 wedges.

5 Divide the salad among six bowls and garnish with the pita wedges.

ROASTED CUMIN: You can streamline this already speedy recipe by subbing out roasted cumin seeds with ground cumin right out of a spice jar. You should need no more than ½ teaspoon in the yogurt dressing.

Nutritional count based on 6 servings (does not include salt and black pepper to taste): 328 calories, 14g protein, 7g fat, 58g carbohydrate, 10g fiber, 638mg sodium

I N MY HUMBLE OPINION, soup doesn't get the respect it deserves. Far too often, it's relegated to a lead-in to the main course or a lazy lunch tipped out of a can. In reality, homemade soup is an economical, fast, healthy, and satisfying meal in its own right. You can stand over a soup pot for half a day if that's the type of cooking you're in the mood for. But you can also achieve great flavor in a soup in less than thirty minutes. And as a bonus, most of the time you can get there by using just one pot.

This soup chapter is like a trip around the world. I love that about soup. I can have it five days in a row and never feel like I'm eating the same thing twice. Let's face it, there's a world of difference between SPICY COCONUT NOODLE SOUP (page 24), LEMONY GREEK CHICKEN SOUP WITH SPINACH (page 38), and BEEFY VIDALIA ONION SOUP (page 36). The first is inspired by Asian takeout, the second derives from a Greek classic, and the third is a sweet Georgia spin on a French classic.

Some of my earliest soup memories are of my aunt Peggy stirring a huge pot that looked like it contained enough to feed an army. I still have the inclination to make soup in big old batches like that. Even if it's just Claudia and me, I'll go right ahead and cook for six, knowing full well I'll have plenty of leftovers. Often I end up eating the soup the next day because I love the way the flavors come together on the second day. Other times, I package up my leftovers in individual servings and pop them in the freezer. That way I've got a quick meal just waiting to be defrosted when I'm short on time.

Of course, if you do have a crowd coming by, soup is a fantastic option for feeding them. Doubling and even tripling soup recipes is generally pretty straightforward—taking a recipe written for four people and stretching it to serve twelve is a simple matter of multiplication. SAUSAGE AND PEPPER POT WITH COLLARD GREENS (page 40) is one of my favorite crowd-pleaser meals. Because it tastes even better with time, getting it done in the morning or even the day before only adds to its flavor and richness. That leaves me free and clear when my guests arrive. All I have to do is heat up the soup on the stove, toss together a simple green salad, and slice up a crusty baguette. Dinner is served.

I may not be able to dedicate several hours to my soups as my wonderful aunt Peggy did, but I love that I'm carrying on the family tradition of making them from scratch. Soups bring fresh ingredients to the table, and home cooking has a way of bringing the whole family together.

2 SOUP SUPPERS

SPICY COCONUT NOODLE SOUP

Asian-style soups are packed full of salty, spicy, and sour flavors that fuse into a winning combination. This one is no exception. Make sure the chili sauce you use has a little sweetness to it so that the flavors really balance out. You can find rice noodles in the international section of most supermarkets, but angel hair pasta will do the trick if you can't get your hands on them. And if shrimp is not your thing, sliced chicken breast is a fine substitution in this satisfying soup.

SERVES 4

4 cups low-sodium chicken broth

½ cup unsweetened coconut milk

2 tablespoons chili sauce, such as
   Heinz chili sauce

Juice of 1 lime

1 teaspoon low-sodium soy sauce

½ pound medium shrimp, peeled and deveined

1 small red bell pepper, thinly sliced

¼ pound snow peas, trimmed

¼ pound thin rice noodles

2 scallions, white and light green parts only,
   chopped

1 In a medium saucepan over medium-high heat, combine the broth, coconut milk, chili sauce, lime juice, and soy sauce and bring to a boil. Add the shrimp, bell pepper, and snow peas, reduce the heat to medium, and simmer until the shrimp are cooked through, about 3 minutes.

2 Meanwhile, in a medium pot of boiling water, cook the rice noodles according to the package directions. Drain well, rinse the noodles under cold water, and drain well again. Divide the noodles among four deep soup bowls.

3 Ladle the soup over the noodles and garnish with the scallions.

Nutritional count based on 4 servings: 298 calories, 19g protein, 10g fat, 34g carbohydrate, 3g fiber, 314mg sodium

LIGHTENED-UP BEER CHEESE SOUP

This classic Wisconsin soup is normally a heart-stopping, cream-laden decadence containing at least twice as many calories as the 223 you'll find in this recipe. That's what makes this incredibly tasty lighter version so darn satisfying. I love that I can indulge in a dish like this simply because I used my smarts to make it more healthful. In the end you get all the great flavors with none of the guilt.

SERVES 6

1 large head cauliflower (about 2 pounds), coarsely chopped

3 large carrots, coarsely chopped

2 celery stalks, coarsely chopped

1 large onion, coarsely chopped

2 garlic cloves, smashed

1 tablespoon olive oil

1 teaspoon salt, plus more to taste

¼ teaspoon cayenne pepper

1 bottle (12 ounces) light mild-flavored beer

4 cups low-sodium chicken or vegetable broth, plus more to taste

1 can (12 ounces) fat-free evaporated milk

1¾ cups shredded low-fat sharp Cheddar cheese, plus more for serving

2 teaspoons Worcestershire sauce

2 tablespoons Dijon mustard

1 teaspoon hot sauce, plus more for serving

Air-popped popcorn, for serving

1 In a food processor (or using a knife), finely chop the cauliflower, carrots, celery, onion, and garlic, working in batches if necessary.

2 Place a large pot or Dutch oven over high heat and add the oil, chopped vegetables, salt, and cayenne. Cook until the vegetables begin to soften, about 5 minutes. Add the beer and broth. Cook until the vegetables are very tender, about 15 minutes more.

3 Transfer the soup to a blender or food processor and puree until smooth (or use an immersion blender to puree right in the pot). Return the soup to the pot and add the evaporated milk, Cheddar, Worcestershire, mustard, and hot sauce. Add more broth if you feel the soup needs to be thinned out, and taste for seasoning. Serve garnished with popcorn, and with more hot sauce and Cheddar if you like.

TIME SAVER: When there's a lot of chopping involved in a meal, I turn to my handy food processor. Not everyone has the lightning-fast knife skills of a professional chef, but with a food processor, you can make quick work of chopping vegetables.

Nutritional count based on 6 servings (does not include Cheddar, hot sauce, and popcorn for serving):
223 calories, 18g protein, 5g fat, 23g carbohydrate, 5g fiber, 933mg sodium

QUICK VEGETABLE MINESTRONE

Most days, I simply don't have the time to invest in slow-cooked soups. Luckily I can always turn to speedy recipes like this easy minestrone. It's chock-full of fresh vegetables, making it a great source of vitamins and minerals. When tomatoes and zucchini aren't in season, I whip up a winter version by subbing in canned tomatoes and bagged spinach. **SERVES 6**

1 small onion

1 carrot

2 garlic cloves

1 tablespoon olive oil

¾ teaspoon salt

1 teaspoon freshly ground black pepper

1 small zucchini (6 ounces), chopped

1½ cups cherry tomatoes (½ pound), halved

8 cups low-sodium vegetable broth

1 can (15½ ounces) cannellini beans, rinsed and drained

3 sprigs fresh basil

¼ cup grated Parmesan cheese

1 In a food processor (or using a knife), finely chop the onion, carrot, and garlic.

2 In a large pot or Dutch oven, heat the oil over medium-low heat. Add the onion, carrot, and garlic and cook, stirring, until the onion and carrot soften but do not brown, about 8 minutes. Season with the salt and pepper. Add the zucchini and tomatoes, and stir to combine. Cook until the zucchini softens slightly, about 3 minutes.

3 Pour in the broth, and add the beans and basil sprigs. Increase the heat to medium, bring to a simmer, and then reduce the heat back to medium-low. Simmer until the soup is slightly thickened, about 15 minutes.

4 Remove and discard the basil sprigs just before serving, and sprinkle with the Parmesan cheese.

Nutritional count based on 6 servings: 165 calories, 8g protein, 4g fat, 25g carbohydrate, 6g fiber, 734mg sodium

PASTA AND BEAN SOUP WITH PESTO

This satisfying soup is helped along by a swirl of good-quality store-bought pesto, so I can enjoy it any time of year. It also happens to be one good-looking bowl of soup, which means it's perfect for days when I've got company. **SERVES 6**

1 teaspoon olive oil

2 garlic cloves, smashed

4 cups low-sodium vegetable broth

1 can (15½ ounces) cannellini beans, rinsed and drained

2 small sprigs fresh rosemary

2 cups small whole-grain pasta shells

½ teaspoon salt

2 tablespoons jarred or prepared pesto

3 tablespoons grated Parmesan cheese

1 In a large pot or Dutch oven, heat the oil over medium heat. Add the garlic and cook, stirring, until fragrant but not browned, about 2 minutes. Add the broth, beans, and rosemary sprigs, and bring to a simmer. Cook for 5 minutes. Add the pasta, increase the heat to medium-high, and bring to a boil. Cook, stirring occasionally, until the pasta is just tender, 10 to 12 minutes.

2 Season with the salt, and use a slotted spoon to remove the garlic cloves and rosemary sprigs. Ladle the soup into bowls, and swirl 1 teaspoon of the pesto into each serving. Sprinkle with the Parmesan, and serve.

Nutritional count based on 6 servings: 210 calories, 9g protein, 4g fat, 32g carbohydrate, 6g fiber, 573mg sodium

SOUTHWEST CORN CHOWDER

Seasonal fresh corn makes this soup thick and satisfying, but it's good to know that I can make it all year round using frozen corn as well. The bell peppers, cayenne, and Cheddar lend a real authentic Southwestern flavor to the chowder. If you've got some cooked chicken in the fridge, go on ahead and throw that in at the end to make it a complete dinner. Or create a vegetarian meal by serving this chowder with my *Mushroom Spinach Quesadillas* (page 111). **SERVES 4**

2 teaspoons canola oil

1 onion, coarsely chopped

1 red bell pepper, coarsely chopped

1 green bell pepper, coarsely chopped

3 scallions

1 pound new potatoes, coarsely chopped

2 cups fresh or frozen corn kernels (10 ounces), thawed if frozen

½ teaspoon salt

¼ teaspoon freshly ground black pepper

⅛ teaspoon cayenne pepper

1 cup 1% milk

½ cup shredded low-fat sharp Cheddar cheese

1 In a large pot or Dutch oven, heat the oil over medium heat. Add the onion and bell peppers. Coarsely chop the white and light green parts of the scallions and add them to the pot (reserve the dark green parts). Cook, stirring, until the vegetables have softened, about 5 minutes. Add the potatoes, half of the corn, 2 cups of water, and the salt, black pepper, and cayenne. Bring to a boil, cover the pot, and reduce the heat to low. Simmer until the potatoes are tender, 10 to 15 minutes.

2 Meanwhile, in a blender, combine the remaining corn and the milk and blend until smooth.

3 Stir the corn-milk puree into the soup and cook until heated through, about 5 minutes.

4 Finely chop the dark green parts of the scallions. Just before serving, sprinkle the scallions and Cheddar over the soup.

Nutritional count based on 4 servings: 250 calories, 12g protein, 1g fat, 44g carbohydrate, 6g fiber, 433mg sodium

BLACK BEAN AND TURKEY SAUSAGE SOUP

I am such a big fan of black bean soup, y'all. There is so much to love in its smoky, spicy flavor, creamy texture, and bright lime finish that I just can't get enough of it. One busy day I had a hankering for this soup so bad, but I had no-where near the time to cook down a ham hock. So I gave it a whirl with some turkey sausage I had on hand. Holy smokes, was I glad I gave it a try. **SERVES 4**

¾ pound Jimmy Dean's Turkey Sausage Crumbles or other cooked turkey sausage with casings removed

1 large onion, chopped

1 large green bell pepper, chopped

1 jalapeño, seeds and veins removed, finely chopped

½ teaspoon salt, plus more to taste

½ teaspoon freshly ground black pepper

3 garlic cloves, finely chopped

1 teaspoon chili powder

1½ cups low-sodium chicken broth

1 can (14½ ounces) chopped tomatoes, with juices

1 teaspoon Worcestershire sauce

2 cans (15½ ounces each) no-salt-added black beans, rinsed and drained

¼ cup chopped fresh cilantro leaves and tender stems

Lime juice to taste

Thinly sliced scallions, dark green parts only, for garnish (optional)

Greek yogurt, for garnish (optional)

Shredded low-fat Cheddar cheese, for garnish (optional)

1 In a large pot, brown the sausage over medium-high heat for about 5 minutes, breaking it up with the back of your spoon. Stir in the onion, bell pepper, jalapeño, salt, and pepper. Cook, stirring, until the onion softens, about 5 minutes. Stir in the garlic and chili powder and cook for 1 minute.

2 Add the broth, tomatoes and juices, and Worcestershire, scraping up any browned bits on the bottom of the pot. Stir in the beans, turn the heat to high, and bring to a boil. Then lower the heat to medium and simmer for 10 minutes. Taste, and adjust the salt if needed.

3 Stir in the cilantro and cook until the soup has thickened, about 5 minutes more. Stir in the lime juice. If you like, serve the soup garnished with the scallions, yogurt, and Cheddar.

SOME LIKE IT HOT: If you prefer your soup with a good spicy kick, leave in the seeds and veins of the jalapeño. Just make sure you warn your guests!

Nutritional count based on 4 servings and using Jimmy Dean's Turkey Sausage Crumbles (does not include lime juice to taste, and scallions, Greek yogurt, and Cheddar cheese for garnish):
343 calories, 30g protein, 8g fat, 39g carbohydrate, 13g fiber, 927mg sodium

LENTIL AND SWISS CHARD SOUP

Because dried lentils are the kind of bean you can cook without soaking first, this soup is super fast and requires no advance planning. And yet it comes out looking like a made-from-scratch soup that you slaved over for hours. Now, I call that genius. I also call it absolutely delicious. And so will you! **SERVES 6**

6 cups low-sodium chicken or vegetable broth

1 can (14½ ounces) diced tomatoes with juices

1 cup dried small brown lentils

1 tablespoon dried minced onion

¾ teaspoon dried rosemary, crumbled

⅛ teaspoon garlic powder

1 bay leaf

1 bunch Swiss chard (about ½ pound), stems removed and leaves coarsely chopped

1 cup instant brown rice

1 teaspoon balsamic vinegar

Freshly ground black pepper to taste

¼ cup grated Parmesan cheese

2 tablespoons olive oil

1 In a medium soup pot over medium-high heat, combine the broth, tomatoes and juices, lentils, minced onion, rosemary, garlic powder, and bay leaf, and bring to a boil.

2 Add the Swiss chard, cover, reduce the heat to medium-low, and simmer for about 20 minutes, until the lentils are nearly tender. Stir in the rice, vinegar, and pepper, cover, and cook for 5 minutes. Remove from the heat, remove and discard the bay leaf, and serve topped with the Parmesan and drizzled with the oil.

CUT IT OUT: When you are using leafy greens like Swiss chard, mustard greens, or collards, it's important to remove the tough inner stem. Here's what you need to do to make quick work of prepping these veggies: First, thoroughly rinse your greens to get rid of any dirt. Lay the leaves flat on a cutting board and, using a knife, cut out the tough stem by slicing along either side of the stem. Stack the trimmed leaves on top of each other and roll them up like a cigar. Then slice or chop according to the recipe directions.

Nutritional count based on 6 servings (does not include black pepper to taste): 291 calories, 17g protein, 8g fat, 40g carbohydrate, 12g fiber, 316mg sodium

CURRIED SWEET POTATO SOUP

I love the brilliant orange color of this warming soup. Topped with a bright white dollop of lemony sour cream, it makes for a real pretty presentation at the table. It's so pretty, in fact, that I don't save this just for quick midweek meals—I also like to make it when I'm having company over. It works as a first course or as a light entrée accompanied by a simple green salad. **SERVES 4**

1 onion
2 celery stalks
1 carrot
1 garlic clove
2 teaspoons olive oil
1 fresh thyme sprig
2 large sweet potatoes (about 1½ pounds), peeled and finely chopped
4 cups low-sodium vegetable broth
1 teaspoon curry powder
⅛ teaspoon cayenne pepper
½ teaspoon salt
¾ teaspoon freshly ground black pepper
½ cup light sour cream
1 teaspoon fresh lemon juice

1 In a food processor (or using a knife), chop the onion, celery, carrot, and garlic.

2 In a large pot or Dutch oven, heat the oil over medium heat. Add the onion, celery, carrot, and garlic and cook, stirring, until the onion softens but does not brown, about 8 minutes.

3 Stir in the thyme sprig and cook for 30 seconds. Add the sweet potatoes, broth, and curry powder and bring to a boil over medium-high heat. Lower the heat to medium and simmer until the sweet potatoes are tender, about 20 minutes. Transfer the soup to a blender or food processor and puree until smooth (or use an immersion blender to puree right in the pot). Return the soup to the pot and season with the cayenne, salt, and ½ teaspoon of the black pepper.

4 In a small bowl, whisk together the sour cream, lemon juice, and remaining ¼ teaspoon black pepper. Ladle the hot soup into bowls and spoon a dollop of the sour cream mixture on top of each.

Nutritional count based on 4 servings: 188 calories, 3g protein, 6g fat, 30g carbohydrate, 5g fiber, 485mg sodium

BEEFY VIDALIA ONION SOUP

I give this French bistro classic a Southern twist by using Vidalia onions. These onions are so sweet, even when they are raw, that you can get them to tender perfection in the blink of an eye. With the addition of lean sirloin, the soup becomes a filling meal on its own. I brown the steak first, then add it back into the soup just near the end of the cooking time. If you prefer your steak more rare, you can skip adding it back into the soup pot and simply place it in the individual serving bowls and ladle the soup over the top. **SERVES 4**

¾ pound lean sirloin steak, trimmed of excess fat
Salt and freshly ground black pepper
1 tablespoon olive oil
2 Vidalia onions, very thinly sliced (about 5 cups)
2 teaspoons light brown sugar
1 tablespoon all-purpose flour
1 tablespoon dry sherry
2 sprigs fresh thyme
4 cups low-sodium beef broth
½ whole-wheat demi baguette (2½ ounces), sliced into 8 rounds
2 slices light Swiss cheese, each cut into 4 squares
Chopped fresh parsley, for garnish

1 Position an oven rack 6 inches from the heat and preheat the broiler to medium-high.

2 Season the sirloin all over with salt and pepper to taste. Heat a wide, deep soup pot over high heat. When the pan is very hot, add the sirloin and cook for 3 minutes on each side. Transfer the meat to a cutting board, tent it with aluminum foil, and let it rest while you prepare the soup.

3 Reduce the heat under the soup pot to medium. Add the oil and onions and cook, stirring, for 5 minutes. Reduce the heat to medium-low, add the brown sugar, stir to coat the onions all over, cover, and cook for 5 minutes.

4 Add the flour, sherry, and thyme sprigs and cook, stirring, for 30 seconds. Add the broth and 2 cups of water, cover, and bring to a boil over medium-high heat. When the soup has come up to a boil, uncover the pot, reduce the heat to medium, and simmer for 5 minutes.

5 Meanwhile, place the bread slices on a sheet of aluminum foil and top each with a square of the cheese. Place them under the broiler until the cheese is melted and the bread is lightly toasted, 1 to 2 minutes.

6 Thinly slice the sirloin (it will be pretty rare still) into 1- to 2-inch-long slices, and add them to the soup along with any accumulated juices. Season the soup to taste with salt and pepper, and cook for 1 to 2 minutes more to warm through. Remove and discard the thyme sprigs. Serve the soup topped with the cheesy bread and garnished with the chopped parsley.

Nutritional count based on 4 servings (does not include salt and black pepper to taste and parsley for garnish):
347 calories, 26g protein, 13g fat, 31g carbohydrate, 4g fiber, 256g sodium

MANHATTAN CLAM CHOWDER

Filming my show *Not My Mama's Meals* up in New York City has had its advantages. I've been discovering all the great foods that New York has given to the rest of us here in the States. Bagels with cream cheese and smoked salmon have become a bit of a guilty habit, and New York pizza is not to be missed. But on the healthier side, I've become a real fan of Manhattan clam chowder. This version is fresh and full of vegetables and cooks in no time at all. **SERVES 4**

1 onion
2 celery stalks
1 carrot
2 garlic cloves
2 teaspoons olive oil
1 bottle (8 ounces) clam juice
1 pound new potatoes, chopped
1 can (28 ounces) whole tomatoes,
    coarsely chopped, with juices
1 bay leaf
2 sprigs fresh thyme
½ teaspoon salt
1 teaspoon freshly ground black pepper
4 pounds small hard-shell clams,
    such as littlenecks, scrubbed well
2 tablespoons coarsely chopped fresh parsley

1 In a food processor (or using a knife), finely chop the onion, celery, carrot, and garlic.

2 In a large pot or Dutch oven, heat the oil over medium-low heat. Add the onion, celery, carrot, and garlic and cook, stirring, until the vegetables soften but do not brown, about 7 minutes.

3 Add 3 cups of water and the clam juice, potatoes, tomatoes and juices, bay leaf, thyme sprigs, salt, and pepper and bring to a boil over medium-high heat. Lower the heat to medium and simmer until the potatoes are tender, about 15 minutes. Lower the heat to medium-low, stir in the clams, and cover the pot. Cook, stirring occasionally, until the clams have opened, 6 to 8 minutes.

4 Discard any unopened clams. Remove and discard the bay leaf and thyme sprigs, and sprinkle with the parsley before serving.

NEW YORK, NEW YORK: Don't confuse Manhattan clam chowder with the creamy variety they serve up in New England. While I love that version as well, this tomato-based chowder tends to be a lot healthier.

Nutritional count based on 4 servings: 207 calories, 13g protein, 3g fat, 33g carbohydrate, 5g fiber, 674mg sodium

LEMONY GREEK CHICKEN SOUP WITH SPINACH

The eggs give this soup a light, creamy consistency and a velvety texture. That's why it seems so very decadent. Why, if I didn't know any better, I'd think there was a carton of cream in here! The lemon juice helps to keep it all nice and light so that you won't feel too weighed down after a bowl of this Greek-style down-home chicken noodle soup. **SERVES 4**

6 cups low-sodium chicken broth

½ cup whole-grain orzo pasta

2 cups chopped fresh spinach

1 cup (5 ounces) chopped cooked chicken breast

3 large eggs, at room temperature

¼ cup fresh lemon juice

Freshly ground black pepper

1 **In a medium soup pot over medium-high heat, bring the broth to a boil. Add the orzo and cook for about 1 minute less than the package directs. Add the spinach and chicken, and simmer until the spinach is wilted, about 2 minutes. Remove from the heat.**

2 **In medium bowl, whisk together the eggs and lemon juice until frothy. Take a ladleful of the hot broth and, whisking constantly, slowly pour it into the egg mixture. Repeat with a second ladleful of broth (don't worry if a few pieces of chicken or spinach wind up in there as well). Then pour the egg mixture into the pot of soup and stir until warmed through. Season to taste with pepper, and serve.**

TEMPER TEMPER: You might be curious as to why I have you pour some of the hot soup into the egg mixture before adding the egg mixture to the soup. Well, let me clear that up. That whole process is called *tempering*. What you're doing is bringing the eggs closer to the temperature of the hot soup before mixing them into the pot. This step ensures that your eggs won't scramble as they hit the simmering broth.

Nutritional count based on 4 servings (does not include black pepper to taste): 216 calories, 20g protein, 5g fat, 19g carbohydrate, 1g fiber, 188mg sodium

HOMEY CHICKEN NOODLE SOUP

Nothing can rival my Mama's homemade chicken noodle soup. But it sure is a time investment. When I don't have hours to devote to soup making and still have a hankering for a homemade-tasting chicken noodle soup, this quick recipe is guaranteed to satisfy. **SERVES 4**

4 cups low-sodium chicken broth

1 celery stalk, sliced

1 carrot, sliced

1 small onion, finely chopped

3 garlic cloves, finely chopped

2 cups whole-wheat egg noodles

1½ cups cubed cooked chicken breast

Salt and freshly ground black pepper

2 tablespoons chopped fresh parsley

1 In a medium pot, combine the broth, 1 cup of water, celery, carrot, onion, and garlic. Simmer over medium heat until the vegetables are tender, about 20 minutes.

2 Stir in the noodles and cook until tender, about 5 minutes. Stir in the chicken and cook until heated through. Season to taste with salt and pepper. Sprinkle with the parsley just before serving.

Nutritional count based on 4 servings (does not include salt and black pepper to taste): 223 calories, 27g protein, 3g fat, 21g carbohydrate, 2g fiber, 151mg sodium

SAUSAGE AND PEPPER POT WITH COLLARD GREENS

One of my all-time favorite treats is a good old Italian-American sausage and peppers sandwich. It's not exactly fare for a healthy midweek meal, so I set myself the task of creating a dish that had all the flavor of that classic sandwich without the heavy load of calories and fat. The result was this delicious one-pot meal. The addition of collards makes it a hearty, nutritional option that's a dead ringer for a decadent indulgence. **SERVES 4**

2 teaspoons olive oil

1 pound turkey sausage,
    sliced into ½-inch-thick rounds

2 large red bell peppers, thinly sliced

2 large green bell peppers, thinly sliced

1 large onion, halved and thinly sliced

½ teaspoon salt

2 garlic cloves, finely chopped

1 small bunch collard greens (about 10 ounces),
    stems removed and leaves sliced

6 cups low-sodium chicken broth

Freshly ground black pepper

Hot sauce, for serving

1 In a large pot over high heat, heat 1 teaspoon of the oil. When the oil is hot, add the sausage. Cook, stirring occasionally, until the sausage is browned all over and cooked through, about 5 minutes. Using a slotted spoon, transfer the sausage to a paper-towel-lined plate.

2 Add the remaining 1 teaspoon oil, the red and green bell peppers, onion, and salt to the pot. Cook until the vegetables have softened, 7 to 8 minutes. Add the garlic and cook until fragrant, about 1 minute. Add the collard greens and cook until slightly wilted, about 2 minutes. Return the sausage to the pot and add the broth. Simmer for 10 minutes. Season with black pepper to taste, and serve with the hot sauce.

Nutritional count based on 4 servings (does not include black pepper and hot sauce for serving):
324 calories, 32g protein, 14g fat, 20g carbohydrate, 6g fiber, 1083mg sodium

WHILE THERE ARE PEOPLE OUT THERE who shy away from cooking fish, I encourage you to add seafood to your regular repertoire because most of it cooks in no time flat, making it a perfect option for a weeknight meal. And it tastes so good when it's prepared simply. All it takes is a few minutes in a hot pan with some salt, pepper, and olive oil and a squirt of lemon to finish it off.

If cooking fish in a pan is outside your culinary comfort zone, cooking it in the oven produces equally delicious results. ROASTED HERBED SALMON (page 60) is as foolproof a recipe as there is: Just place the fillets in a baking dish, cover them with an herb mixture, and pop the dish in the oven.

Living in Savannah, I have access to some of the freshest fish you can find. So my daily commute home often includes stopping off at the fish market for the fresh catch of the day. But if you live in a slightly more landlocked area, frozen seafood is a great option. It defrosts quickly and loses not one ounce of its great flavor from the freezing process. Even though I can get fantastic fresh shrimp, I always keep a bag of frozen shrimp on hand in case I get a last-minute hankering for SHRIMP AND RICE (page 44) or GARLICKY BAKED SHRIMP (page 50).

Seafood can also be bought in a can. My pantry is stocked with cans of good-quality tuna so that I have the supplies on hand to make SPICY TUNA PASTA WITH OLIVES AND TOMATOES (page 51), one of Claudia's favorite dishes. She treats me right back by cooking LEMON-MUSTARD TUNA STEAKS (page 58). Since I like my tuna on the rare side and she likes to serve it with a simple fresh salad, this particular dinner can be on the table in about five minutes flat.

Truth be told, though, my favorite way to get the ingredients for a good seafood dinner is to get out into nature and catch it myself. When you know exactly where your food started out, you can't help but appreciate it more. For years now, Jack and I have gone on frequent uncle-nephew fishing expeditions, oftentimes from the end of my dock out back. I have to say, for a little tyke, he's pretty darn good. And he's always so proud to contribute to the family meal. Yes sir, he sure is a Deen boy through and through.

Whether you get your seafood fresh from the market, frozen, canned, or just-caught out of the water, there is an option that's just right for you. I ought to know. I come from a family that never met a piece of meat they didn't like. And just look at me now: spreading the gospel of the bounties of the sea.

SHRIMP AND RICE

This quick stir-fry is based on Savannah's traditional Red Rice with Shrimp, a dish that gets its brilliant color from ripe red tomatoes. In my version, the tomatoes are joined by spicy cayenne pepper and smoky paprika. If it's flavor you're seeking, look no further. This meal will wake up your taste buds and fill your belly, a fully satisfying plate of food. **SERVES 4**

½ cup white rice
1 tablespoon olive oil
1 onion, coarsely chopped
1 red bell pepper, coarsely chopped
1 garlic clove, chopped
1 pound large shrimp, peeled and deveined
Juice of 1 lemon
½ teaspoon salt
½ teaspoon smoked paprika or sweet paprika
⅛ teaspoon cayenne pepper
3 plum tomatoes (¾ pound), coarsely chopped
¼ cup finely chopped fresh parsley

1 In a medium saucepan, stir together the rice and 1 cup of water. Bring to a boil, then cover the pan and reduce the heat to low. Simmer until the rice is tender and the liquid has been absorbed, about 18 minutes. Remove the pan from the heat, fluff with a fork, and keep covered.

2 Meanwhile, in a large skillet, heat the oil over medium-low heat. Add the onion, bell pepper, and garlic and cook, stirring, until the onion has softened, about 5 minutes. Stir in the shrimp, lemon juice, salt, paprika, and cayenne and cook, stirring, until the shrimp begin to turn pink, about 1 minute. Add the tomatoes and cook, stirring, until they begin to break down, 2 to 3 minutes. Sprinkle with the parsley, and serve the shrimp over the rice.

Nutritional count based on 4 servings: 276 calories, 26g protein, 6g fat, 29g carbohydrate, 3g fiber, 464mg sodium

LIGHT AND EASY SCALLOPS AND GRITS

I always cook scallops in butter. Call it an indulgence I just won't give up. On the other hand, I think grits cooked with skim milk cook to creamy perfection, no heavy cream necessary! Little trade-offs like this make it possible for me to maintain a balanced diet. I encourage you to find your own trade-offs so that you can more easily stick to a healthy diet. Eating right should feel like good choices, not deprivation. **SERVES 4**

1 cup skim milk
½ teaspoon salt
½ teaspoon freshly ground black pepper
⅓ cup quick-cooking grits (not instant)
2 teaspoons shredded extra-sharp white
   Cheddar cheese
2 tablespoons thinly sliced scallions,
   white and light green parts only
1¼ pounds large sea scallops (about 16 scallops)
1 tablespoon unsalted butter
Tabasco sauce, for serving

1 In a medium saucepan, combine the milk, 1 cup of water, ¼ teaspoon of the salt, and ¼ teaspoon of the pepper, and heat over medium-high heat until the mixture is almost boiling. Reduce the heat to low and slowly whisk in the grits. Cook, stirring frequently with a wooden spoon, until the grits are thick and creamy, 4 to 5 minutes. Stir in the Cheddar and two-thirds of the scallions. Remove from the heat, cover the pan, and let stand while you cook the scallops.

2 Pat the scallops dry with a paper towel and season them with the remaining ¼ teaspoon salt and ¼ teaspoon pepper. In a medium skillet, melt the butter over medium-high heat. Once the butter is hot and bubbling, add the scallops and sear, turning them once, until golden brown on both sides and just cooked through, about 5 minutes.

3 Serve the scallops on top of the grits, sprinkled with the remaining scallions and drizzled with Tabasco.

THE TRUTH ABOUT BUTTER: While butter gets a bad rap because of its fat content, it's worth pointing out that it actually contains far fewer calories than olive oil. A tablespoon of butter tops out at 100 calories, while a tablespoon of olive oil is around 130 calories.

Nutritional count based on 4 servings (does not include Tabasco for serving): 225 calories, 27g protein, 5g fat, 17g carbohydrate, 0g fiber, 558mg sodium

SHRIMP COCONUT CURRY

Dried curry powder is a great shortcut to huge flavor. This Indian curry dish manages to be hearty and filling while at the same time light and bright. Claudia loves this meal and could eat it just about once a week, so I switch out the ingredients to change it up each time. Sometimes I use chicken and sometimes I keep it vegetarian by subbing in eggplant and mushrooms. But this shrimp version is my favorite, and I think it's the winner, hands down. **SERVES 4**

1 tablespoon vegetable oil

1 onion, chopped

1 garlic clove, chopped

½ cup low-sodium chicken broth

½ cup unsweetened coconut milk

2 teaspoons curry powder

2 teaspoons cornstarch

1 pound large shrimp, peeled and deveined

1 teaspoon fresh lemon juice

Salt and freshly ground black pepper

Hot cooked rice, for serving

2 tablespoons toasted coconut flakes,
  for serving

1 In a large skillet, heat the oil over medium-high heat. Add the onion and cook until softened, about 5 minutes. Reduce the heat to medium, add the garlic, and cook for 30 seconds, until fragrant. Add the broth, coconut milk, and curry powder and stir to combine.

2 In a small bowl, combine the cornstarch with 2 teaspoons of water and stir until dissolved.

3 Stir the cornstarch mixture into the curry sauce and bring to a boil. Cook, stirring constantly, until thickened, about 1 minute. Add the shrimp and lemon juice and cook until the shrimp are cooked through, 2 to 3 minutes. Season to taste with salt and pepper. Serve over the rice, with the coconut flakes sprinkled on top.

· ·
Nutritional count based on 4 servings (does not include salt and black pepper to taste or rice and coconut flakes for serving): 244 calories, 25g protein, 13g fat, 8g carbohydrate, 1g fiber, 181mg sodium

CRAB AND SHRIMP CAKES WITH CORN RELISH

These seafood cakes are Savannah cooking through and through. My Mama's husband, Michael, is the king of crab and shrimp cakes like these, and I learned everything I know about them from him. Just to make it a total family affair, I use my Mama's awesome House Seasoning in the mix. This is Deen family cooking at its best. **SERVES 4**

1 cup fresh or frozen corn kernels,
   thawed if frozen
1 cup chopped red bell pepper
1 scallion, light and dark green parts only,
   chopped
1 teaspoon fresh lime juice
1 teaspoon plus 1 tablespoon canola oil
Salt and freshly ground black pepper
½ pound cooked crabmeat, picked over to
   remove any bits of shell
5 ounces shelled cooked shrimp
   (from ½ pound raw), finely chopped
⅓ cup panko breadcrumbs
1 large egg
1 tablespoon light mayonnaise
1 teaspoon grated fresh ginger
1 teaspoon Dijon mustard
¼ teaspoon Paula Deen's House Seasoning
   (recipe follows)
¼ teaspoon hot sauce, or to taste
Mixed lettuce leaves, for serving

1 In a medium bowl, toss together the corn, bell pepper, scallion, lime juice, the 1 teaspoon oil, and salt and pepper to taste.

2 In a second medium bowl, toss together the crab, shrimp, and breadcrumbs.

3 In a small bowl, whisk the egg with the mayonnaise, ginger, mustard, House Seasoning, and hot sauce. Pour the egg mixture over the crab mixture and, using a spoon, mix gently until just combined.

4 In a large nonstick skillet, heat the remaining 1 tablespoon oil over medium heat. Form the crab mixture into 8 patties and cook, turning them once, until browned on both sides, about 5 minutes in total. Serve the crab and shrimp cakes on a bed of mixed greens, topped with the corn relish.

Nutritional count based on 4 servings (does not include lettuce for serving or salt and black pepper to taste):
326 calories, 40g protein, 10g fat,
18g carbohydrate, 2g fiber, 822mg sodium

PAULA DEEN'S HOUSE SEASONING

This simple spice mix is a must for any spice cabinet and makes just about anything taste better.

Makes 1½ cups
1 cup salt
¼ cup freshly ground black pepper
¼ cup garlic powder

Combine all the ingredients in a bowl. Store in an airtight container for up to 6 months.

GARLICKY BAKED SHRIMP

My new favorite way to cook shrimp is to bake it in the oven at a high temperature. I have found this method to be flat-out foolproof. The shrimp always come out juicy and tender and it takes almost no time at all! This baked shrimp is exploding with great garlic flavor, a hint of spiciness, and a nice tangy finish. A simple vegetable dish such as my *Broiled Herbed Mushrooms* (page 154) rounds out this meal just perfectly. **SERVES 4**

1 pound medium shrimp, peeled and deveined
6 garlic cloves, thinly sliced
2 tablespoons dry white wine
2 teaspoons olive oil
Pinch of crushed red pepper flakes
½ teaspoon salt
¼ cup dried whole-wheat breadcrumbs
2 tablespoons finely chopped fresh parsley,
    plus more for serving
Lemon wedges, for serving

1 Preheat the oven to 425°F.

2 In a medium bowl, combine the shrimp, garlic, wine, 1 teaspoon of the oil, the red pepper flakes, and ¼ teaspoon of the salt. Scrape into a medium-size baking dish.

3 In a small bowl, combine the breadcrumbs, parsley, and the remaining 1 teaspoon oil and ¼ teaspoon salt. Sprinkle the breadcrumb mixture over the shrimp, and bake until the shrimp are opaque, 10 to 12 minutes. Serve garnished with more parsley and with lemon wedges for squeezing over the top.

Nutritional count based on 4 servings (does not include lemon and parsley for serving): 178 calories, 24g protein, 5g fat, 8g carbohydrate, 0g fiber, 507mg sodium

SPICY TUNA PASTA WITH OLIVES AND TOMATOES

If you can get your hands on a good-quality canned tuna for this dish, you will have the makings of a real special meal. I'm talking true date-night cooking. In fact, I remember making this dish for Claudia not long before I asked her to marry me. Now that I think of it, I reckon it worked in my favor. **SERVES 6**

1 pint cherry tomatoes, halved

Pinch of salt plus ½ teaspoon

1 box (13¼ ounces) whole-grain pasta, such as penne, fusilli, or rigatoni

2 teaspoons olive oil

1 garlic clove, finely chopped

½ cup pitted green olives, thinly sliced

¼ teaspoon crushed red pepper flakes, plus more for serving (optional)

2 cans (5 ounces each) tuna packed in water, drained

Juice of 1 lemon

⅓ cup chopped fresh basil, plus more for serving

1 In a small bowl, stir the tomatoes with the pinch of salt. Let the tomatoes sit to soften slightly.

2 In a large pot of boiling salted water, cook the pasta according to the package directions. Drain the pasta, reserving ½ cup of the pasta water.

3 In a medium skillet, heat the oil over high heat. Add the garlic, tomatoes, olives, red pepper flakes, reserved pasta water, and the remaining ½ teaspoon salt. Cook, stirring, until the tomatoes are very soft and the sauce has thickened, about 6 minutes.

4 Add the pasta, tuna, lemon juice, and basil. Toss to combine, and adjust the seasonings to taste. Serve garnished with more basil and red pepper flakes, if you like.

Nutritional count based on 6 servings (does not include extra red pepper flakes and basil for serving):
326 calories, 24g protein, 5g fat, 50g carbohydrate, 1g fiber, 612mg sodium

FISH TACOS WITH AVOCADO PICO DE GALLO

Something about fish tacos makes me feel like I've just gone on an island vacation. On a Tuesday or Wednesday night during the dark winter months, that's always a nice feeling to capture. So I tend to make these tacos on stormy, chilly evenings when I want to make myself half believe I'm sitting on a sunny beach. They're fresh, bright tasting, and just the right amount of spicy. **SERVES 4**

1¼ pounds mild white fish fillets,
    such as tilapia or catfish
1 teaspoon Old Bay Seasoning
½ teaspoon salt, plus more to taste
¼ teaspoon freshly ground black pepper
Hot sauce (optional)
2 tablespoons finely chopped red onion
1 pint cherry tomatoes, quartered
Juice of 1 lime
¼ cup loosely packed fresh cilantro leaves,
    chopped
½ avocado, pit removed
2 teaspoons olive oil
8 corn tortillas (6-inch diameter)
Shredded lettuce or green cabbage, for serving

1 Cut each fish fillet into 1-inch-wide slices. Place the fish in a medium bowl and sprinkle with the Old Bay Seasoning, ¼ teaspoon of the salt, the pepper, and a few dashes of hot sauce if you are using it. Toss to coat the fish and let it sit at room temperature for 10 minutes.

2 Meanwhile, in a medium bowl, combine the onion, tomatoes, lime juice, cilantro, and remaining ¼ teaspoon salt. Using a sharp knife, cut into the flesh of the avocado vertically and horizontally to make cubes. Use a spoon to remove the cubes from the skin. Add to the tomato mixture and stir to combine. Taste, and add more salt if you think it needs it.

3 Heat a medium nonstick skillet over medium-high heat. Once it is hot, add 1 teaspoon of the oil and cook half of the fish for 2 to 3 minutes per side, until just cooked through. Place on a plate and repeat with the remaining oil and fish. Tent the plate with aluminum foil.

4 Place the tortillas on a microwave-safe plate and cover them with a damp paper towel. Warm in the microwave for 30 seconds to 1 minute, until pliable and soft.

5 Divide the fish among the tortillas. Top with the avocado-tomato salsa, some lettuce or cabbage, and more hot sauce if you like.

MAKE IT A TEX-MEX FEAST: For a Tex-Mex–themed dinner party, pair this dish with some baked tortilla chips and salsa and shots of Southwest Corn Chowder (page 27). Mix up some margaritas and let the fiesta begin!

Nutritional count based on 4 servings (does not include hot sauce or lettuce/cabbage for serving):
307 calories, 32g protein, 9g fat, 28g carbohydrate, 5g fiber, 391mg sodium

FETTUCCINE WITH WHITE CLAM SAUCE

If you can't make it to southern Italy, here's a dish that will bring you there in spirit. This scrumptious pasta dish is so surprisingly decadent that it's hard to believe it's as fantastically healthy as it is. It's one of my buddy Sam's favorites. Because he works out so much, he has a notorious appetite, so when I serve it to him, I make sure I round out the meal with a hearty salad to start things off and some crusty bread for sopping up the sauce. **SERVES 4**

1 tablespoon olive oil

2 garlic cloves, finely chopped

½ teaspoon crushed red pepper flakes, or more to taste

½ cup dry white wine

2 cans (6 ounces each) chopped clams, drained and juices reserved

Grated zest and juice of 1 lemon

¼ teaspoon salt

½ teaspoon freshly ground black pepper

½ pound whole-grain fettuccine

1 teaspoon unsalted butter

2 tablespoons finely chopped fresh parsley

1 In a large skillet, heat the oil over medium-low heat. Add the garlic and cook until softened, about 2 minutes. Add the red pepper flakes and cook until fragrant, about 30 seconds. Add the wine, increase the heat to medium-high, and bring to a boil. Cook until the wine has almost completely evaporated, 5 to 7 minutes. Lower the heat, add the clam juice, and stir to combine. Cook for 1 minute. Then add the clam meat, lemon zest, and lemon juice. Season with the salt and pepper.

2 Meanwhile, in a large pot of boiling salted water, cook the pasta until just tender, 8 to 10 minutes. Drain the pasta, reserving ½ cup of the pasta water.

3 Add the butter to the clam sauce, stirring until combined. Add the pasta to the clam sauce and toss to coat, adding a few teaspoons of the pasta water if needed. Transfer to a serving bowl, sprinkle with the parsley, and serve.

Nutritional count based on 4 servings: 271 calories, 9g protein, 5g fat, 46g carbohydrate, 0g fiber, 334mg sodium

PAN-FRIED TILAPIA WITH CAJUN BUTTER

Because this homemade Cajun butter is so rich and flavorful, a little goes a long way. Just be sure to get that butter on top of the fish when the fish is still good and hot so that it melts all over it. Just thinking about this tasty dish sets my mouth to watering. **SERVES 4**

3 tablespoons unsalted butter,
    at room temperature
2 tablespoons fresh lemon juice
1 teaspoon finely chopped fresh parsley
¼ teaspoon Cajun spice blend
¾ teaspoon freshly ground black pepper
4 tilapia fillets (5 ounces each)
½ teaspoon salt
2 teaspoons canola oil

1 In a small bowl, combine the butter, 1 tablespoon of the lemon juice, the parsley, Cajun spice blend, and ¼ teaspoon of the pepper.

2 Pat the tilapia dry with paper towels and season on both sides with the salt and the remaining ½ teaspoon black pepper.

3 In a large skillet, heat the oil over medium-high heat. Add the tilapia and cook until golden on one side, about 3 minutes. Carefully flip the fillets over and cook until they are flaky and just cooked through, 2 to 3 minutes. Sprinkle with the remaining 1 tablespoon lemon juice and serve with the Cajun butter.

COMPOUND INTEREST: The Cajun butter in this recipe is an example of a French cooking element called compound butter. You can flavor butters with just about any spice, herb, or booze. All you have to do is get the butter to the soft room temperature stage and then mix in the flavoring of your choice. If you are not using the butter right away, you can re-form it into a log, wrap it in plastic wrap, and chill it or freeze it. Cut off slices to add to meats, vegetables, and fish. And remember, a little goes a long way.

Nutritional count based on 4 servings: 234 calories, 28g protein, 13g fat, 1g carbohydrate, 0g fiber, 365mg sodium

RED SNAPPER WITH OLIVES, TOMATOES, AND CAPERS

I've found that fish cooked in a tomato sauce like this always comes out tender and juicy. This Mediterranean-inspired dish is pretty much foolproof cooking. And that's exactly the kind of cooking I need after a busy day of work—don't you, too? Tack on a side serving of *Creamy Spinach Polenta* (page 177) to create a restaurant-worthy weekday meal. **SERVES 4**

1 tablespoon vegetable oil

2 garlic cloves, chopped

3 tomatoes (about 1 pound), chopped

¼ cup pitted green olives, sliced crosswise

1 tablespoon capers, rinsed and drained

¼ teaspoon dried oregano

Salt and freshly ground black pepper

4 red snapper or other firm-fleshed
   white fish fillets (about 5 ounces each)

In a large skillet, heat the oil over medium-high heat. Add the garlic and cook until fragrant, about 30 seconds. Add the tomatoes, olives, capers, and oregano and cook, stirring frequently, until the tomato juices begin to evaporate, about 3 minutes. Season the sauce with salt and pepper to taste. Add the fish and cook, turning once, until a fork inserted into the thickest part of a fillet meets no resistance, about 5 minutes in total.

....
Nutritional count based on 4 servings (does not include salt and black pepper to taste): 213 calories, 30g protein, 8g fat, 5g carbohydrate, 2g fiber, 376mg sodium

LEMON-MUSTARD TUNA STEAKS

Anyone who knows me knows that tuna is by far my favorite fish. And Claudia certainly knows me well. I credit her with the inspiration for this simple yet stunning recipe. She made a version of this dish for me one night and I flipped for it, kind of like I flipped for her. It really is true that the quickest way to a man's heart is through his stomach. **SERVES 4**

2 tablespoons Dijon mustard

2 teaspoons whole-grain mustard

Grated zest and juice of 1 lemon

4 tuna steaks (6 ounces each)

½ teaspoon salt

½ teaspoon freshly ground black pepper

1 tablespoon canola oil

1 In a small bowl, whisk together the Dijon mustard, whole-grain mustard, and lemon zest.

2 Season the tuna steaks with the salt and pepper, and spread the mustard mixture all over them.

3 In a large skillet, heat the oil over medium-high heat. Add the tuna and cook, turning it once, until browned outside and medium-rare inside, about 2 minutes per side. Drizzle with the lemon juice and serve immediately.

Nutritional count based on 4 servings: 225 calories, 40g protein, 6g fat, 2g carbohydrate, 1g fiber, 467mg sodium

BROILED GROUPER WITH HERBED CROUTONS

Grouper is a firm white fish with a nice mild flavor. It's the perfect fish to serve next to something with lots of herby flavor. These homemade croutons are so darn good and they make a perfect complement to this subtle fish. On top of all that, it looks so nice on the plate. Tuck a lemon wedge on each plate and it looks so good—you're in your own fancy restaurant! **SERVES 4**

1 small whole-wheat baguette (5 ounces) or
   half a regular one, sliced in half lengthwise
1 garlic clove, halved
3 teaspoons olive oil
1 tablespoon finely chopped fresh basil
1 tablespoon finely chopped fresh parsley
1 teaspoon finely chopped fresh chives
1 teaspoon freshly ground black pepper
4 grouper fillets (6 ounces each)
½ teaspoon salt
Lemon wedges, for serving

1 Preheat the oven to 400°F.

2 Rub the cut sides of the bread with the cut sides of the garlic clove. Chop the bread into ½-inch pieces. In a medium bowl, toss the bread cubes with 2 teaspoons of the oil and the basil, parsley, chives, and ½ teaspoon of the pepper. Transfer the cubes to a baking sheet and bake until they are golden and crisp, 6 to 8 minutes. Transfer to a medium bowl and use a paper towel to wipe down the baking sheet.

3 Preheat the broiler.

4 Place the grouper fillets on the baking sheet and season with the salt and the remaining ½ teaspoon pepper. Drizzle with the remaining 1 teaspoon oil, and broil until the grouper is just cooked through, 5 to 7 minutes. Serve the grouper with the croutons scattered over the top and lemon wedges on the side.

CRAZY FOR CROUTONS: These herbed croutons are great in so many dishes. I sprinkle them on top of soups, toss them into salads, and add them to cheese platters. I usually make more than I need for this dish and keep them fresh in an airtight container for up to a week. If I've got them on hand, I use them in my *Grilled Chicken Caesar Salad* (page 129).

Nutritional count based on 4 servings (does not include lemon wedges for serving): 210 calories, 34g protein, 5g fat, 5g carbohydrate, 0g fiber, 433mg sodium

ROASTED HERBED SALMON

It really doesn't matter what mix of fresh herbs you use on roasted salmon, but here's the combination that happens to be my favorite right now: parsley, basil, and chives. To create a complete meal, pair this dish with *Roasted Brussels Sprouts* (page 147) and white or brown rice. **SERVES 4**

4 skinless salmon fillets (6 ounces each)
¾ teaspoon salt
1 teaspoon freshly ground black pepper
¼ cup finely chopped fresh parsley
¼ cup finely chopped fresh basil
2 tablespoons finely chopped fresh chives
1 garlic clove, finely chopped
2 tablespoons olive oil
Lemon wedges, for serving

1 Preheat the oven to 425°F.

2 Season the salmon fillets with the salt and pepper. In a small bowl, mix together the parsley, basil, chives, garlic, and oil. Spread the herb mixture over the salmon fillets and place them in a 9-inch square baking dish.

3 Roast until the fish is flaky and almost cooked through, 12 to 15 minutes. Remove the dish from the oven, cover it loosely with aluminum foil, and let the salmon rest for 10 minutes before serving it with plenty of lemon wedges.

....
Nutritional count based on 4 servings (does not include lemon wedges for serving): 349 calories, 36g protein, 21g fat, 1g carbohydrate, 0g fiber, 518mg sodium

STIR-FRIED SHRIMP AND VEGGIES

The key to successful stir-fry cooking is to have all your ingredients chopped and ready by the stove before you get cooking. Once you heat the oil in the wok, it's game on because dinner is mere minutes away. It's fast, it's fun, and it's super tasty. Now that's *my* kind of cooking. **SERVES 4**

2 tablespoons low-sodium soy sauce

2 tablespoons low-sodium chicken broth

2 teaspoons cornstarch

1 teaspoon rice vinegar

1 teaspoon sugar

½ teaspoon garlic powder

¼ teaspoon ground ginger

Pinch of crushed red pepper flakes

2 tablespoons peanut or canola oil

¼ pound snow peas, trimmed

1 red bell pepper, cut into 2-inch-long strips

4 scallions: dark green parts chopped, white and light green parts cut into 1-inch pieces

1 pound medium shrimp, peeled and deveined

1 can (8 ounces) sliced bamboo shoots, drained

1 can (8 ounces) whole baby corn, drained

1 In a small bowl, combine the soy sauce, broth, cornstarch, vinegar, sugar, garlic powder, ginger, and red pepper flakes. Stir until the cornstarch has dissolved.

2 In a wok or large skillet, heat the oil over high heat. Add the snow peas and bell pepper and cook, stirring constantly, for 1 minute. Add the 1-inch scallion pieces and the shrimp and cook, stirring constantly, until the shrimp begin to curl, 1 to 2 minutes. Add the bamboo shoots, baby corn, and soy sauce mixture and stir until the shrimp are cooked through, about 2 minutes. Serve garnished with the chopped scallion greens.

....

Nutritional count based on 4 servings: 299 calories, 28g protein, 10g fat, 26g carbohydrate, 5g fiber, 685mg sodium

FOR MOST PEOPLE I KNOW, poultry, and in particular chicken, is a mainstay of their workweek menus, and for good reason! When it comes to chicken, you can walk into any supermarket in the country and find a wide array of cuts from which to choose. On the one hand, there is the lean white meat of the hen, which is versatile and tasty and can be cooked quickly. On the other is the more indulgent dark meat from the thigh and leg, which is juicy, flavorful, and fantastically economical. But what's really great about chicken is the seemingly endless ways that it can be prepared. A date night in with Claudia might feature a sophisticated dish like PAN-FRIED CHICKEN CUTLETS WITH MUSHROOMS AND WHITE WINE (page 79), while a casual backyard picnic with the guys might be better suited to PEACHY PULLED BBQ CHICKEN (page 66). Both are prepared using boneless, skinless chicken breasts, but the resulting dishes are worlds apart.

I don't limit myself to white meat, though. Thighs and drumsticks are so delicious that you don't have to do much to make a truly tasty meal out of them. ROASTED LEMON-OLIVE CHICKEN THIGHS (page 69) is a great example of that. When you are starting with a juicy cut like chicken thighs, lemon and olive oil are just about all you need to cook up a finger-licking meal.

Another great lean poultry that cooks in no time flat is turkey. Whether you go for ground meat or thin-sliced cutlets, the important thing to remember with turkey is not to overcook it. I like to serve this meat with a flavorful sauce, like the marinara in TURKEY MEATBALLS WITH 10-MINUTE MARINARA (page 80) or the chicken broth and sherry–based sauce drizzled over TURKEY CUTLETS FLORENTINE (page 83).

I have become a true convert to ground turkey over ground beef. Sure, ground beef still has a place in my diet, but I do love that I can easily cut calories and fat by substituting ground turkey, or by mixing half a quantity of ground turkey with half a quantity of ground beef. When I'm looking to splurge a little, that's how I make my TURKEY SLOPPY JOES (page 82), but honestly, most nights I make them using ground turkey alone and I don't miss the beef a bit.

I don't know one person who doesn't like a good old chicken or turkey dish. Poultry just seems to be universally loved and a regular weeknight go-to. Whether it's pan-fried, braised, or roasted, it's something most folks come together on. I love when food has a way of doing that.

GREEN CHICKEN CHILI

Green chili stew is Southwest comfort food at its finest. My friends from Texas and New Mexico seem to always have a pot of this stew bubbling away on the stove. The smell is so inviting and the taste even better. This version of the classic one-pot meal comes together in under 30 minutes and has about half the usual amount of calories. That's midweek cooking I can feel good about. **SERVES 6**

1 teaspoon olive oil
1 large onion, finely chopped
1 large green bell pepper, finely chopped
2 garlic cloves, finely chopped
1 pound lean ground chicken
1 tablespoon chili powder
1 teaspoon ground cumin
1 teaspoon dried oregano
¼ teaspoon cayenne pepper
1 teaspoon salt, plus more to taste
2 cans (4 ounces each) chopped green chiles
1 cup fresh or frozen corn kernels,
    thawed if frozen
4 cups low-sodium chicken broth
2 cans (15½ ounces each) low-sodium Great
    Northern beans, rinsed and drained
½ cup chopped fresh cilantro,
    plus more for serving
Lime wedges, for serving
Hot sauce, for serving
Corn tortilla chips, for serving

1 In a large pot, heat the oil over high heat. Add the onion and bell pepper and cook until almost tender and beginning to brown, about 7 minutes. Add the garlic and cook for 30 seconds.

2 Add the ground chicken, chili powder, cumin, oregano, cayenne, and salt. Cook, breaking up the chicken with a spoon, until it is cooked through and beginning to brown, 4 to 5 minutes.

3 Add the chiles, corn, and broth and bring to a boil. Reduce the heat to medium and simmer for 10 minutes.

4 Add the beans and cook until heated through, about 2 minutes. Stir in the cilantro. Check the seasoning, and add more salt if you think it needs it. Serve garnished with more cilantro, as well as lime wedges, hot sauce, and tortilla chips, if you like.

CHILE CHOICE: New Mexico green chiles are the chiles you're looking for in this recipe. You can find cans of them in the international section of most supermarkets. They tend to be mild yet flavorful. Most of them come from Hatch, New Mexico, the self-proclaimed "Chile Capital of the World."

Nutritional count based on 6 servings (does not include extra cilantro, lime, hot sauce, and corn tortilla chips for serving):
318 calories, 26g protein, 9g fat, 37g carbohydrate, 11g fiber, 885mg sodium

PEACHY PULLED BBQ CHICKEN

It doesn't get more down-home and Southern than this plate of food. Peachy barbecue chicken is Georgia through and through. I tested this recipe on my Mama, the Queen of Southern Food, and she gave it two thumbs up. I rounded out the meal by serving it with my *Lemony Cabbage Slaw* (page 158) and a tall, cold glass of iced tea. She was so darn proud. **SERVES 6**

2 large boneless, skinless chicken breasts
   (½ pound each), halved crosswise
2 boneless, skinless chicken thighs (¼ pound
   each), trimmed of excess fat
½ teaspoon salt
½ teaspoon freshly ground black pepper
1 tablespoon olive oil
3 ripe peaches (about 1¼ pounds), peeled,
   pits removed, and coarsely chopped
1 cup bottled barbecue sauce
1½ teaspoons hot sauce
Juice of 1 lemon
6 whole-wheat hamburger buns, split open

1 Place the chicken breasts and thighs on a plate and pat dry with a paper towel. Season the chicken with the salt and pepper.

2 In a large pot or Dutch oven, heat the oil over medium heat. Add the peaches and cook, stirring, until they soften but do not brown, 5 to 7 minutes. Add the chicken pieces and stir to coat. Pour in ½ cup of water and the barbecue sauce, hot sauce, and lemon juice. Stir to combine, making sure the chicken pieces are covered completely (add more water if necessary). Increase the heat to medium-high, bring to a boil, and then reduce the heat to medium-low. Simmer, uncovered, until the sauce thickens and the chicken is cooked through, 12 to 15 minutes.

3 Remove the pot from the heat. Transfer the chicken pieces to a cutting board and use two forks to shred the meat. Return the shredded meat to the pot and stir to combine.

4 Serve the peachy pulled chicken in between the hamburger bun halves.

Nutritional count based on 6 servings: 294 calories, 17g protein, 6g fat, 44g carbohydrate, 3g fiber, 924mg sodium

QUICK JERK CHICKEN

For a taste of the islands, nothing beats jerk chicken. This spicy, flavorful concoction will make you feel as if you have just landed in the Caribbean. I like to serve this quick chicken dish with my *Mango Salsa* (page 97) and a simple scoop of brown rice. It's like a midweek vacation! **SERVES 6**

2 tablespoons vegetable oil

2 tablespoons fresh lime juice

2 scallions, white and light green parts only, chopped

1 Scotch bonnet pepper, seeded and chopped (or substitute 1 jalapeño, seeded and chopped)

1 garlic clove, chopped

1 teaspoon ground allspice

1 teaspoon dried thyme

1 teaspoon low-sodium soy sauce

1 teaspoon browning seasoning, such as Gravy Master (available in the spice section of most supermarkets)

¼ teaspoon freshly ground black pepper

Salt to taste

1½ pounds boneless, skinless chicken thighs, trimmed of excess fat

1 Position an oven rack 6 inches from the heat and preheat the broiler to high. Grease a rimmed baking sheet with cooking spray.

2 In a blender, combine the oil, lime juice, scallions, Scotch bonnet, garlic, allspice, thyme, soy sauce, browning seasoning, and pepper. Blend until almost smooth; then taste the sauce and season it with salt if you think it needs it.

3 In a large bowl, toss the chicken with the sauce. Transfer the chicken to the prepared baking sheet and broil until cooked through, about 5 minutes per side.

BONNET BURN: If you do use a Scotch bonnet in this recipe, a word of warning is in order: These pretty little peppers are deceptively hot. I always use gloves when working with them, and I pretty much always take out the seeds. Unless you really want to feel the burn, I recommend you follow these simple precautions too.

Nutritional count based on 6 servings (does not include salt to taste): 185 calories, 22g protein, 9g fat, 3g carbohydrate, 0g fiber, 127mg sodium

ROASTED LEMON-OLIVE
CHICKEN THIGHS

The olives in this speedy dish crisp up in the oven to provide a nice contrast to the tender, juicy chicken thighs. All in all, this meal is super quick, super tasty, and super satisfying. **SERVES 4**

4 boneless, skinless chicken thighs
 (¼ pound each), trimmed of excess fat
2 teaspoons olive oil
½ teaspoon dried oregano
½ teaspoon salt
½ teaspoon freshly ground black pepper
Finely grated zest and juice of 1 lemon
¼ cup pitted green olives, thinly sliced

1 Preheat the oven to 425°F.

2 While the oven is heating, combine the chicken, oil, oregano, salt, pepper, lemon zest, and olives in a medium bowl. Toss to combine and coat, and then let sit until the oven reaches 425°F.

3 Scrape the chicken and olives onto a rimmed baking sheet, making sure the chicken thighs are not too crowded. Roast until the chicken is cooked through, 15 to 18 minutes. Transfer to a plate, tent it with aluminum foil, and let the chicken rest for 5 minutes. Serve sprinkled with the lemon juice.

. . . .
Nutritional count based on 4 servings: 132 calories, 17g protein, 6g fat, 2g carbohydrate, 1g fiber, 417mg sodium

OVEN-FRIED CHICKEN PO'BOYS

I'm nuts about po'boys, whether they are made with oysters, shrimp, fish, or chicken. But the traditional deep-fried sandwich fillings can be dangerous for the waistline. Luckily you can get really good results by cooking the meat at a high temperature in the oven. Topped with a tangy, spicy light mayonnaise spread and crunchy romaine lettuce leaves, this here sandwich sure does the trick of satisfying my po'boy cravings. **SERVES 4**

¼ cup low-fat buttermilk

1 garlic clove, finely chopped

1 teaspoon Dijon mustard

1 teaspoon hot sauce

Salt and freshly ground black pepper

¾ pound boneless, skinless chicken thighs, each cut in half crosswise

1 cup whole-wheat panko breadcrumbs

¼ cup light mayonnaise

Juice of ½ lemon

4 multigrain wraps (8-inch diameter)

4 romaine lettuce leaves

1 large tomato, sliced into 8 rounds

1 In a large bowl, whisk together the buttermilk, garlic, mustard, ½ teaspoon of the hot sauce, and salt and pepper to taste. Add the chicken and toss to coat. Marinate at room temperature for 5 minutes. (If you have the time, go on ahead and marinate the chicken for longer. Feel free to get the chicken into the marinade the night before if that's easier for you.)

2 Meanwhile, preheat the oven to 400°F.

3 In a large bowl, combine the panko with salt to taste. Line a baking sheet with aluminum foil and set a wire rack on top. Working with one piece at a time, remove the chicken from the buttermilk mixture (allowing the excess to drip off) and dredge the chicken completely in the panko. Transfer the chicken to the wire rack. Grease the chicken lightly with cooking spray and bake until it is cooked through, about 20 minutes.

4 Meanwhile, in a small bowl, whisk together the mayonnaise, lemon juice, and remaining ½ teaspoon hot sauce.

5 When the chicken is done, spread the mayonnaise on one side of the wraps, and top each one with an equal amount of chicken, a lettuce leaf, and 2 slices of tomato. Roll up and serve warm or at room temperature.

CRISP CRUST: Cooking the chicken on a wire rack helps to keep the whole piece nice and crisp. It lends an authentic fried texture by ensuring that the bottom of the chicken pieces don't go all soggy from sitting on the baking sheet.

Nutritional count based on 4 servings (does not include salt and black pepper to taste): 337 calories, 23g protein, 11g fat, 34g carbohydrate, 3g fiber, 560mg sodium

ONE-PAN ROASTED CHICKEN AND BROCCOLI

There's one-pot cooking and now there's one-*pan* cooking. Sweet caramelized broccoli and tender lemony chicken combine here for a bold-flavored meal. And cleaning just one bowl and the one pan sure does make for a quick post-dinner washup, an added bonus on a busy weeknight. **SERVES 4**

2 pounds broccoli, cut into bite-size florets
2 tablespoons olive oil
1 tablespoon low-sodium chicken broth or water
2 garlic cloves, finely chopped
½ teaspoon ground cumin
1 teaspoon salt
1 teaspoon freshly ground black pepper
⅛ teaspoon hot chili powder
1 pound boneless, skinless chicken breasts, cut into 1-inch pieces
1¼ teaspoons finely grated lemon zest (from 1 large lemon)
Lemon wedges, for serving

1 Preheat the oven to 425°F.

2 On a large rimmed baking sheet, combine the broccoli with 1 tablespoon of the oil, the broth or water, half of the garlic, the cumin, ½ teaspoon of the salt, ½ teaspoon of the pepper, and the chili powder. Toss to coat, and then spread the broccoli out into a single layer. Roast for 10 minutes.

3 Meanwhile, in a large bowl, combine the chicken, remaining 1 tablespoon oil, remaining garlic, the lemon zest, remaining ½ teaspoon salt, and remaining ½ teaspoon pepper. Toss to coat.

4 Remove the baking sheet from the oven, add the chicken, and toss together with the broccoli. Return the sheet to the oven and roast, tossing once halfway through the cooking time, until the chicken is cooked through and the broccoli is tender and golden around the edges, 8 to 10 minutes.

5 Serve with the lemon wedges, or squeeze the lemon juice all over the chicken and broccoli just before serving.

Nutritional count based on 4 servings (does not include lemon wedges for serving): 270 calories, 32g protein, 12g fat, 13g carbohydrate, 7g fiber, 690mg sodium

BROILED PINEAPPLE-LIME DRUMSTICKS

Be sure to pass 'round the napkins with this meal. It's the kind of eating that makes it worth getting messy. The sweet and tangy basting sauce is lip-smacking, finger-lickin' delicious. **SERVES 4**

¼ cup pineapple preserves
1 tablespoon fresh lime juice
1 tablespoon teriyaki sauce
Pinch of cayenne pepper
8 chicken drumsticks (¼ pound each), skin removed
Salt and freshly ground black pepper

1 Position an oven rack 6 inches from the heat and preheat the broiler to medium. Line a rimmed baking sheet with aluminum foil and grease the foil with cooking spray.

2 In a blender or small food processor, puree the preserves, lime juice, teriyaki sauce, and cayenne until smooth. Place 2 tablespoons of this sauce in a small bowl and set it aside. Place the remaining mixture in a second small bowl.

3 Season the drumsticks lightly with salt and pepper, and place them on the pre-pared baking sheet. Using a basting brush, brush the tops of the drumsticks with the pineapple mixture in the second small bowl. Broil, turning and brushing with the pineapple mixture every 5 minutes, until cooked through, 15 to 20 minutes.

4 Wash the basting brush thoroughly (to avoid cross-contamination), and brush the reserved 2 tablespoons pineapple sauce over the cooked drumsticks before serving.

Nutritional count based on 4 servings (does not include salt and black pepper to taste): 149 calories, 16g protein, 3g fat, 15g carbohydrate, 0g fiber, 244mg sodium

SPICED CHICKEN THIGHS WITH SPINACH

This dish perfectly illustrates how a lean, simple dinner can be made exciting by loading it up with spices. I love this chicken served over basmati rice or with a piece of toasted naan bread. **SERVES 4**

4 boneless, skinless chicken thighs (¼ pound each), trimmed of excess fat and sliced into ½-inch-wide strips

1 teaspoon curry powder

⅛ teaspoon cayenne pepper

⅛ teaspoon ground cinnamon

1 garlic clove, finely chopped

½ teaspoon salt

½ teaspoon olive oil

1 red onion, thinly sliced

1 package (10 ounces) frozen spinach, thawed and squeezed of excess liquid

Juice of ½ lemon

1 In a medium bowl, sprinkle the chicken strips with the curry powder, cayenne, cinnamon, garlic, and ¼ teaspoon of the salt. Toss well, and let it marinate for 5 minutes.

2 In a large skillet over high heat, heat the oil until shimmering. Add the chicken and onion and cook, stirring occasionally, for 8 minutes or until the chicken is cooked through and the onion is tender. Add the spinach, the remaining ¼ teaspoon salt, and the lemon juice. Cook for 2 minutes to warm through. Then transfer to a platter and serve.

Nutritional count based on 4 servings: 174 calories, 25g protein, 5g fat, 7g carbohydrate, 3g fiber, 440mg sodium

STIR-FRIED CHICKEN WITH GREEN BEANS AND CASHEWS

When I order Chinese takeout for a quiet night in, this dish is almost always on my list. While I love it, you can bet it's a good bit more fattening than I really care to know. More often than not, I whip up my own healthy yet incredibly tasty version. And the funny thing is, it actually takes me less time to cook this meal than it takes to have it delivered! **SERVES 4**

½ pound green beans, trimmed and cut into
   2-inch pieces
2 tablespoons low-sodium soy sauce
1 tablespoon low-sodium chicken broth
1 teaspoon rice vinegar
1 teaspoon cornstarch
½ teaspoon Sriracha or other chili sauce
1 tablespoon peanut or canola oil
2 teaspoons chopped fresh ginger
2 garlic cloves, chopped
1 pound boneless, skinless chicken breasts,
   cut into 1-inch pieces
⅓ cup roasted, salted cashews

1. Bring a medium pot of salted water to a boil over high heat. Add the green beans and cook for 2 minutes, until crisp-tender. Drain and run under cold water to cool down, then drain again.

2. In a small bowl, combine the soy sauce, broth, vinegar, cornstarch, and Sriracha and stir until the cornstarch has dissolved.

3. In a wok or large skillet, heat the oil over high heat. Add the ginger and garlic and cook, stirring constantly, for 10 seconds. Add the chicken and cook, stirring constantly, until no trace of pink remains on the surface. Add the green beans and the soy sauce mixture and cook, stirring constantly, until the chicken is cooked through, about 2 minutes. Stir in the cashews and serve.

Nutritional count based on 4 servings:
246 calories, 29g protein, 10g fat,
9g carbohydrate, 2g fiber, 293mg sodium

PAN-FRIED CHICKEN CUTLETS WITH MUSHROOMS AND WHITE WINE

This fancy-looking yet simple dinner is a great excuse to crack open a nice bottle of wine. Use a little in the sauce and set out the rest to enjoy with the meal. Maybe light a candle or two and bring out the good china while you tell yourself it's Saturday night when it's actually only Tuesday. I guarantee you'll be halfway to believing it by the second bite in. **SERVES 4**

2 tablespoons olive oil

4 boneless, skinless thin-sliced chicken cutlets
(6 ounces each)

½ teaspoon salt

½ teaspoon freshly ground black pepper

2 garlic cloves, smashed

4 cups (10 ounces) sliced baby bella or shiitake
mushrooms

2 fresh thyme sprigs

½ cup dry white wine

½ cup low-sodium chicken broth

3 tablespoons finely chopped fresh parsley

1 In a large skillet, heat 1 tablespoon of the oil over medium heat. Season the chicken with ¼ teaspoon of the salt and ¼ teaspoon of the pepper. Add the chicken to the skillet and cook until golden brown on one side, about 5 minutes. Flip the chicken and cook until golden on the second side, about 3 minutes. Transfer the chicken to a plate.

2 Add the remaining 1 tablespoon oil and the garlic to the skillet and cook, stirring, until the cloves are fragrant and lightly browned, about 2 minutes. Add the mushrooms and thyme sprigs and continue to cook, stirring, until the mushrooms are tender,

about 5 minutes. Pour in the wine and use a wooden spoon to scrape up any browned bits from the bottom of the pan. Stir in the broth and bring to a simmer. Cook until the sauce is reduced by half, 5 to 7 minutes.

3 Season the sauce with the remaining ¼ teaspoon salt and ¼ teaspoon pepper. Return the chicken and any accumulated juices to the pan, add 2 tablespoons of the parsley, and stir to coat the chicken all over.

4 Remove the garlic cloves and thyme sprigs. Sprinkle the remaining tablespoon of parsley over the chicken just before serving.

EVERYTHING IN MODERATION: A typical glass of white wine has about 120 calories, and those calories do not have any nutritional value. That fact alone is enough to keep me away from alcohol on most nights. Keeping my weight under control is just one of many good reasons I choose to drink in moderation.

Nutritional count based on 4 servings:
239 calories, 42g protein, 2g fat,
6g carbohydrate, 1g fiber, 417mg sodium

TURKEY MEATBALLS WITH 10-MINUTE MARINARA

It may sound too good to be true, but this 10-minute marinara is the real deal. You'll be happily surprised by its intense flavor. And the Pecorino Romano–filled meatballs are no slouches in the flavor department, either. I love finding a fast route to big taste. Serve these meatballs with a heaping plate of steamed or sautéed spinach or some whole-grain pasta. **SERVES 6**

MARINARA

1 tablespoon olive oil

2 garlic cloves, smashed

1 can (28 ounces) crushed tomatoes

1 small bunch fresh basil

¼ teaspoon crushed red pepper flakes

¼ teaspoon dried oregano

¼ teaspoon salt

¼ teaspoon freshly ground black pepper

TURKEY MEATBALLS

1 pound 93%-lean ground turkey

2 garlic cloves, finely chopped

1 large egg, lightly beaten

⅓ cup chopped fresh parsley

¼ cup whole-wheat panko breadcrumbs

4 tablespoons grated Pecorino Romano cheese

½ teaspoon salt

¼ teaspoon crushed red pepper flakes

2 tablespoons olive oil

1 Make the marinara: In a medium skillet, heat the oil over medium-high heat. Add the garlic cloves and sauté until fragrant, about 2 minutes. Add the tomatoes, basil, red pepper flakes, oregano, salt, and pepper and simmer, uncovered for 9 minutes.

2 Meanwhile, prepare the meatballs: In a large bowl, mix the turkey, garlic, egg, parsley, panko, 2 tablespoons of the Pecorino, the salt, and the red pepper flakes just to combine. Form into 1-inch round meatballs.

3 In a large skillet, heat the oil over medium-high heat. Add the meatballs and sauté until browned on all sides, about 5 minutes.

4 Add the meatballs to the marinara sauce and simmer until the sauce thickens slightly and the meatballs are heated through, about 10 minutes. Remove the garlic cloves and basil bunch, sprinkle with the remaining 2 tablespoons Pecorino, and serve.

....

Nutritional count based on 6 servings: 285 calories, 20g protein, 17g fat, 14g carbohydrate, 3g fiber, 693mg sodium

TURKEY SLOPPY JOES

In order to get his sons, Jack and Matthew, to eat more vegetables, my brother, Jamie, started adding grated carrots to his burgers. I have to say they are just about the best burgers I've ever tried. It's no wonder my nephews love them! I decided to give this trick a whirl with turkey Sloppy Joes, and it was a huge success. The carrots add sweetness, nutrients, and body to the meat mix without adding extra fat. But beware: This is a four-napkin kind of meal that is a great big fun mess! **SERVES 4**

1 tablespoon olive oil

1 garlic clove, finely chopped

2 large carrots, coarsely grated (about 2 cups)

1 onion, grated

1 pound 93%-lean ground turkey

2¼ cups boxed or jarred strained tomatoes or canned tomato sauce

2 teaspoons cider vinegar

2 teaspoons Worcestershire sauce

¾ teaspoon ground cumin

¾ teaspoon chili powder

¼ teaspoon cayenne pepper, or more to taste

2 whole-wheat hamburger buns, split open

1 In a large, deep skillet, heat the oil over medium-high heat. Add the garlic, carrots, and onion and cook, stirring, until the vegetables have softened, about 4 minutes. Add the turkey and cook, stirring occasionally, until browned, about 5 minutes.

2 Pour in the strained tomatoes or sauce, the vinegar, Worcestershire, cumin, chili powder, and cayenne. Cook, uncovered, until the mixture thickens, about 15 minutes.

3 Divide the meat mixture among the hamburger bun halves, and serve open-faced.

TOP TOMATOES: I prefer to use strained tomatoes in this recipe because I like the consistency for the Sloppy Joe mix and because it doesn't add a lot of sweetness. Strained tomatoes are usually sold in cartons or tall glass bottles in the canned tomato section of the supermarket. If you can't find them, go ahead and use a tomato sauce with little to no sugar added.

Nutritional count based on 4 servings: 322 calories, 24g protein, 14g fat, 26g carbohydrate, 5g fiber, 991mg sodium

TURKEY CUTLETS FLORENTINE

Laid out on a pretty platter, this dish is a dead ringer for fancy restaurant food. But believe me, dinner doesn't come together much quicker than this! Turkey cutlets are delicate pieces of meat that should not be cooked for long—a couple minutes per side and they are done to perfection. If you've got company coming round in the middle of the week, I highly suggest this recipe. You'll be able to spend more time with your guests and less time in the kitchen, while still setting out an impressive centerpiece dish. **SERVES 4**

3 teaspoons olive oil

1½ pounds thinly sliced turkey cutlets (about ¼ inch thick)

Salt and freshly ground black pepper

1 tablespoon unsalted butter

1 large onion, thinly sliced

2 garlic cloves, thinly sliced

¼ cup dry sherry

½ cup low-sodium chicken broth

1 tablespoon capers, rinsed and drained

1 tablespoon finely chopped fresh sage

3 cups packed spinach leaves, coarsely chopped

1 In a large skillet, heat 2 teaspoons of the oil over high heat. Season the turkey with salt and pepper to taste. When the oil is hot, add half of the turkey to the skillet and cook until golden brown on one side, about 2 minutes. Flip the turkey and cook until golden on the second side, about 1 minute. Transfer the turkey to a plate. Add the remaining teaspoon of oil to the skillet and repeat with the remaining turkey.

2 Reduce the heat to medium and add the butter to the skillet. When it has melted, add the onion and cook, stirring, until it is browned and softened, about 8 minutes. (Go ahead and add a little water to the pan if it gets too dry.) Add the garlic and cook for 1 minute. Then add the sherry and cook for 1 minute more. Pour in the broth and bring to a boil. Add the capers, sage, and spinach and stir until the spinach is beginning to wilt, about 2 minutes.

3 Return the turkey cutlets and any accumulated juices to the skillet, cover, and cook for 1 minute to heat through.

4 Arrange the turkey cutlets on a serving platter and pour the spinach, onions, and sauce over the top. Serve immediately.

ITALIAN IDYLL: This northern Italian dish works great in a multicourse dinner party. Start the feast out with my *Quick Vegetable Minestrone* (page 27). Next, serve up appetizer portions of *Fettuccine with White Clam Sauce* (page 54). Cap the meal off with these *Turkey Cutlets Florentine* accompanied by *Easy Parmesan-Crusted Zucchini* (page 112). And if anyone manages to have room for dessert, I recommend a light fruit-based sweet, such as *Minted Berries with Yogurt Cream* (page 182).

Nutritional count based on 4 servings (does not include salt and black pepper for seasoning and to taste):
283 calories, 42g protein, 9g fat, 6g carbohydrate, 1g fiber, 261mg sodium

WHEN I WAS GROWING UP IN ALBANY, GEORGIA, meat was a big part of our family dinners. If it wasn't chicken, you can be sure there was beef or pork on our plates. Because it was economical, dinner was frequently built around ground beef. And Mama found a thousand and one ways to keep it interesting.

Our move to Savannah marked the beginning of a sea change. And I mean that literally! Savannah introduced us to a whole new world of seafood that we hadn't encountered in Albany. Gradually, fish and shellfish became a common weekday meal. More recently, as my family has become increasingly health conscious, veggies and grains have taken on a bigger role in our diet. My, how things have changed.

I never quite lost my love of a good meat-based meal. When done right, it doesn't have to be unhealthy. Whether you dress it up real fancy like CHIPOTLE PORK CHOPS WITH MANGO SALSA (page 97) or keep it super simple like MUSTARD-RUBBED FLANK STEAK (page 86), a meal that offers meat is always satisfying and gratifying.

On weekdays, to keep it fast and easy, I steer away from roasts and cuts of meat that take time to cook down to tenderness. I favor lean, quick-cooking cuts like flank steak and sirloin. I make my Chinese-style BEEF AND BROCCOLI STIR-FRY (page 90) using flank and my Korean-style BEEF LETTUCE WRAPS (page 92) with sirloin. Keeping these cuts on the heat too long toughens them up, making them perfect for speedy stir-frying and broiling.

I haven't forsaken good old affordable ground beef, though. I look forward to nights when I'm cooking PASTA WITH BEEF BOLOGNESE (page 94) or MINI MEAT LOAVES (page 91) just as much as I look forward to a meal featuring prime sirloin. There's something so comforting about a plate of ground beef done right. When I'm eating meat loaf, I can't help but think fondly on my aunt Peggy, who taught me everything I know about this dish.

If I'm craving meat but want something a little healthier than red meat, I choose pork. Tenderloin is just about as lean as you can get. As unbelievable as it may seem, pound for pound it's actually as lean as skinless chicken breast. ROASTED PORK TENDERLOIN WITH ONIONS AND CARROTS (page 95) is spiced with a heady mix of paprika, coriander, oregano, and garlic powder. It tastes and looks exquisitely decadent but tops out at only 216 calories and 7 grams of fat per serving!

And finally, there are pork chops. I love this cut so much that I've included three recipes for it in this chapter! Sauced, braised, or stuffed, pork chops always deliver great flavor. There are so many delicious ways to cook chops and I plan on working my way through all of them.

MUSTARD-RUBBED FLANK STEAK

I made this flank steak for my brother, Jamie, on a recent rainy night and he was bowled over by how good it was. We had been feeling a little sorry for ourselves because it wasn't grilling weather, but this fine piece of meat bucked us right up. It's the perfect mix of sweet, spicy, and salty that really seems to satisfy. **SERVES 4**

1 pound flank steak
2 teaspoons mustard powder
2 teaspoons light brown sugar
¾ teaspoon salt
½ teaspoon freshly ground black pepper
½ teaspoon chili powder
¼ teaspoon ground cumin

1 Position an oven rack 6 inches from the heat and preheat the broiler to high.

2 While the broiler is heating, pat the steak dry with a paper towel. In a small bowl, mix together the mustard powder, brown sugar, salt, pepper, chili powder, and cumin. Rub both sides of the steak with the spice mixture. Let the steak sit at room temperature for 10 minutes.

3 Preheat a cast-iron skillet (or a broiler-safe stainless-steel skillet) on the stove for 2 minutes over medium-high heat. Place the steak in the hot skillet and cook for 2 minutes. Flip the steak, place the skillet under the broiler, and broil for 3 to 5 minutes, until the internal temperature of the steak registers 130°F on an instant-read thermometer for medium-rare. Cook for another couple minutes for medium.

4 Carefully remove the skillet from the oven and place the steak on a plate or platter. Top it with any juices from the skillet, and tent it with aluminum foil. Let the steak rest for 5 to 10 minutes.

5 Slice the steak against the grain and serve topped with the juices.

Nutritional count based on 4 servings: 203 calories, 24g protein, 10g fat, 3g carbohydrate, 0g fiber, 501mg sodium

STEAK TACOS WITH QUICK PICKLED RED ONIONS

I reckon I could live on tacos of all stripes. I love the classic ground beef, the more exotic grilled fish varieties, and the simple, straightforward bean taco. But my favorite has got to be a hearty steak taco. In this one the spice rub brings a touch of heat, the cabbage adds a nice crunchy texture, and the pickled onions and lime lend a bright acidic punch. **SERVES 4**

½ tablespoon ground cumin
1 tablespoon chili powder
½ teaspoon salt, plus more to taste
½ teaspoon freshly ground black pepper
1 pound flank steak
1 tablespoon olive oil
½ small red onion, thinly sliced
Juice of 6 limes (about ¾ cup)
Pinch of sugar, plus more to taste
8 small (4-inch diameter) corn tortillas
2 cups thinly shredded green cabbage
Fresh cilantro leaves, for serving
Hot sauce, for serving

1 In a small bowl, combine the cumin, chili powder, salt, and pepper to create the spice rub. Use a paper towel to pat the flank steak dry, and generously sprinkle the spice rub on both sides. Pour ½ teaspoon of the oil on each side of the steak and rub in the spices. Let the steak sit at room temperature for 10 minutes.

2 Meanwhile, combine the onion, lime juice, sugar, and salt to taste in a bowl. Set aside, stirring occasionally.

3 Heat a medium skillet over high heat and add 1 teaspoon of the oil. When it is hot, add the flank steak and cook on one side, without moving it, for 4 to 5 minutes, until a charred crust forms. Add the remaining 1 teaspoon oil to the pan, flip the steak, and cook the other side for 4 to 5 minutes, until the internal temperature of the steak reaches 130°F on an instant-read thermometer for medium-rare. Cook for another few minutes for medium. If any browned bits begin to burn on the bottom of the pan, splash a little water into the pan. Transfer the steak to a cutting board and let it rest for 10 minutes, loosely covered with aluminum foil.

4 When you are ready to serve the tacos, wrap the tortillas in a slightly damp kitchen towel and microwave on low for 30 seconds, or until warm. Working against the grain, thinly slice the steak and distribute it among the tortillas. Use a colander to drain the red onion pickling liquid into a medium bowl, toss the cabbage in the liquid, and divide it among the tacos. Serve with the pickled red onions, cilantro leaves, and hot sauce on the side.

PICKLING PATIENCE: If you've got the time in the morning, I highly suggest you pickle your red onions ahead of time. Pickled vegetables just get better with age. And be sure you hold on to any leftover onions after this meal. They are great in sandwiches and salads throughout the week.

Nutritional count based on 4 servings (does not include cilantro leaves and hot sauce for serving):
325 calories, 26g protein, 14g fat, 26g carbohydrate, 4g fiber, 418mg sodium

BEEF AND BROCCOLI STIR-FRY

One of the many great things about a quick-cooking stir-fry like this one is that it's best made with the leanest cut of beef you can find. And there's no danger that the meat will be lacking in taste because this soy-ginger marinade is seriously full-flavored. Be sure you slice the beef nice and thin before you add it to the marinade so that the slices get coated all over. **SERVES 4**

1½ tablespoons low-sodium soy sauce
1-inch piece fresh ginger, peeled and grated
1 teaspoon cornstarch
1½ teaspoons canola oil
1 pound beef sirloin, thinly sliced
1 tablespoon rice vinegar
½ teaspoon sugar
1 small head broccoli (about 1 pound), cut into
    bite-size florets
1 garlic clove, finely chopped

1 In a medium bowl, whisk together 1 tablespoon of the soy sauce, the ginger, the cornstarch, and ½ teaspoon of the oil. Add the beef and toss to coat. Marinate at room temperature for 10 minutes.

2 In a small bowl, whisk together the remaining ½ tablespoon soy sauce, the rice vinegar, and the sugar until the sugar dissolves.

3 Into a large skillet or wok, pour enough water to reach 1 inch up the sides of the pan. Bring to a boil over medium-high heat, and add the broccoli. Cover the skillet and cook until the broccoli is tender and bright green, about 3 minutes. Drain the broccoli (discarding the water from the pan) and transfer to a medium bowl.

4 Wipe out the skillet with a paper towel. Place the skillet over high heat and add the remaining 1 teaspoon oil. Once the oil is hot, add the garlic and cook, stirring constantly, until fragrant, 15 seconds. Drain the beef from the marinade, add it in one layer to the skillet, and cook for 30 seconds on one side; then flip and cook for another 30 seconds on the second side. Stir in the soy-vinegar mixture and cook for 30 seconds to 1 minute, until the beef is cooked through. Add the cooked broccoli to the skillet and toss to coat. Serve immediately.

EASY PEEL: Here's a quick restaurant trick for peeling ginger: Using a knife can result in lots of wasted ginger flesh. Surprisingly, the best tool to use is a metal spoon. That's right, a spoon. The skin of the ginger is actually super thin, so all you need to do is scrape the skin with the edge of the spoon and it will come off cleanly, with minimal effort on your part. Don't you just love kitchen shortcuts like that?

Nutritional count based on 4 servings: 290 calories, 33g protein, 13g fat, 10g carbohydrate, 3g fiber, 300mg sodium

MINI MEAT LOAVES

My nephews love these little meat loaves. And I love them too, but not just for their great taste (and believe me, they are hopping with flavor). This particular meat loaf recipe has finally put me in contention for the family meat loaf competition. For years Aunt Peggy held the title for best meat loaf, though Brooke and Jamie have given her a good run for her money. And now I've officially joined the ranks with these tasty bites. May the best loaf win! **SERVES 6**

1½ pounds 95%-lean ground beef

½ cup dried breadcrumbs

¾ cup grated Parmesan cheese

⅓ cup canned tomato sauce

2 large eggs, lightly beaten

3 tablespoons dried minced onion

1 tablespoon whole milk

1 tablespoon Worcestershire sauce

1 teaspoon Paula Deen's House Seasoning (page 49)

½ teaspoon dried basil

½ teaspoon dried marjoram

½ teaspoon dried thyme

2 tablespoons ketchup

1 Preheat the oven to 400°F. Grease a 12-cup muffin tin with cooking spray.

2 In a large bowl, combine the beef, breadcrumbs, ½ cup of the Parmesan, tomato sauce, eggs, minced onion, milk, Worcestershire, House Seasoning, basil, marjoram, and thyme. Use your hands to combine well.

3 Divide the meat mixture evenly among the muffin tin cups. Brush the tops with the ketchup, and sprinkle with the remaining ¼ cup Parmesan. Bake until the loaves are cooked through, about 25 minutes.

Nutritional count based on 6 servings: 282 calories, 33g protein, 11g fat, 11g carbohydrate, 1g fiber, 704mg sodium

BEEF LETTUCE WRAPS

This is such a fun meal to make for a crowd. While this recipe is written for four people, most of the time I double or even triple the amounts and invite a bunch of friends over for an Asian feast. When that's the case, I like to serve these wraps with *Whole-Grain Fried Rice* (page 176) and *Hot Roasted Green Beans with Sweet Chili* (page 155). When it comes to the veggie garnishes, I let my imagination go wild. This combo of carrot, cucumber, and mint is one of my favorites, but the beef also tastes great with sprouts, blanched snow peas, radishes, cilantro, or whatever other vegetables you love best. **SERVES 4**

3 tablespoons low-sodium soy sauce

1 tablespoon toasted sesame oil

1 tablespoon Sriracha or other chili sauce

1 pound top sirloin steak, sliced into ¼-inch-thick strips

¾ cup hot cooked white rice (optional)

8 large red-leaf lettuce leaves

1 carrot, thinly sliced

1 small cucumber (5 ounces), peeled and cut into ¼-inch-thick slices

4 large sprigs fresh mint

1 lime, cut into 8 wedges

1 In a small bowl, whisk together the soy sauce, sesame oil, and Sriracha. Place the beef in a large, shallow bowl, pour the marinade over it, and toss to coat. Let the beef marinate at room temperature for 15 minutes.

2 Position an oven rack 3 inches from the heat and preheat the broiler to high. Grease a rimmed baking sheet with cooking spray.

3 Meanwhile, place the rice (if you are using it) in a small serving bowl. On a large serving platter, arrange the lettuce leaves, carrot and cucumber slices, mint, and lime wedges.

4 Arrange the beef, along with the marinade, in one layer on the prepared baking sheet, and broil until cooked through, 3 to 4 minutes. Transfer the beef to a serving platter. Pour the sauce from the baking sheet into a small serving bowl.

5 Now invite everyone to grab a lettuce leaf, pile on the beef and all of the toppings, drizzle with the sauce, spritz with the lime, roll up the lettuce leaf, and enjoy.

Nutritional count based on 4 servings: 335 calories, 26g protein, 18g fat, 17g carbohydrate, 2g fiber, 510mg sodium

PASTA WITH BEEF BOLOGNESE

I refuse to believe that a hearty plate of pasta bolognese is strictly for weekends. And this little recipe here proves that I got it right. When I don't have the time to simmer a sauce for hours, I whip up this quick meaty one. Its deep rich flavor will surprise and delight you. **SERVES 6**

2 teaspoons olive oil
1 strip turkey bacon, thinly sliced crosswise
1 onion, finely chopped
1 teaspoon salt
½ teaspoon freshly ground black pepper
2 garlic cloves, finely chopped
¾ pound 95%-lean ground beef
½ teaspoon dried oregano
Pinch of ground cinnamon
1 can (28 ounces) chopped tomatoes, with juices
¼ cup chopped fresh parsley, plus more for serving
1 package (13¼ ounces) whole-grain spaghetti

1 Bring a large pot of salted water to a boil for the pasta.

2 Meanwhile, in a medium skillet over high heat, cook the oil and bacon for about 2 minutes, until the bacon begins to brown and crisp. Add the onion, salt, and pepper and cook until the onion is beginning to soften, about 3 minutes. Add the garlic and cook for 1 minute more.

3 Add the ground beef to the pan, along with the oregano and cinnamon. Cook, breaking the meat up with a wooden spoon, until no pink remains, about 5 minutes.

4 Add the tomatoes and parsley. Simmer the sauce on medium-high heat, stirring occasionally, for 15 minutes or until it is slightly reduced and has turned a deep red color.

5 Meanwhile, add the pasta to the boiling water and cook according to the package directions.

6 Drain the pasta well, place it in a serving bowl, and top with the sauce. Sprinkle with more parsley, and serve.

THE WHOLE TRUTH: If you just aren't into whole-grain spaghetti, you can always prepare this recipe using regular spaghetti. The two types actually have about the same number of calories. However, if it's carbs you're watching, I don't recommend using regular white-flour pasta because it's made up of simple carbohydrates. This type of carb can be broken down by your body and turned into sugar much more quickly than the complex variety in whole-grain pasta. And the quicker your body gets the sugar, the less chance it has to burn it off and the more likely it is to be turned into fat.

Nutritional count based on 6 servings (does not include parsley for serving):
346 calories, 23g protein, 6g fat, 54g carbohydrate, 2g fiber, 665mg sodium

ROASTED PORK TENDERLOIN WITH ONIONS AND CARROTS

Roasted pork tenderloin in 30 minutes? Yes, it's possible! To help this juicy, tender meat cook a little quicker, I cut the tenderloins into three pieces. Smaller roasts equal less cooking time. I always end up slicing my tenderloin before I serve it anyway, so this makes no difference in the presentation. I think sweet carrots are a nice partner to pork, and roasting carrots is the best way to draw out every bit of their natural sweetness. **SERVES 6**

2 tablespoons smoked paprika

2 teaspoons ground coriander

1 teaspoon dried oregano

1 teaspoon garlic powder

1 teaspoon salt

¼ teaspoon freshly ground black pepper

2 pork tenderloins (about 1 pound each), each cut into 3 pieces

1 tablespoon olive oil

1 large onion, thinly sliced

3 large carrots, cut on the diagonal into 1-inch pieces

1 Preheat the oven to 425°F. Line a baking sheet with aluminum foil, and lightly grease it with cooking spray.

2 In a small bowl, stir together the paprika, coriander, oregano, garlic powder, salt, and pepper. Pat the pork pieces dry with a paper towel. Sprinkle the spice rub all over the pork, pressing on it so it adheres.

3 Transfer the pork to the prepared baking sheet, and roast until the internal temperature reaches 145°F on an instant-read thermometer, about 20 minutes.

4 Meanwhile, in a large skillet, heat the oil over medium heat. Add the onion and carrot and cook, stirring, until the onion is beginning to soften, about 5 minutes. Scrape the vegetables onto the baking sheet holding the tenderloins, arranging them around the meat, and continue to roast for the final 15 minutes of the pork cooking time.

5 Transfer the onion and carrots to a large serving platter. Let the pork rest, tented with foil, for 5 minutes before slicing it and serving it on top of the onion and carrots.

Nutritional count based on 6 servings: 216 calories, 31g protein, 7g fat, 8g carbohydrate, 2g fiber, 772mg sodium

CHIPOTLE PORK CHOPS WITH MANGO SALSA

The sweet and tangy mango salsa I serve with this dish goes great with the smoky, spicy chipotle rub on the chops. I love this recipe when fresh summer mangos are at their sweetest. Enjoying this dinner outside on a warm Savannah evening is like finding a little bit of heaven on earth. Try the *Zucchini Corn Fritters* (page 156) with this main. They taste out of this world topped with the mango salsa. **SERVES 4 / MAKES 2 CUPS MANGO SALSA**

MANGO SALSA

2 small mangoes (about 1¼ pounds), cut into
  ½-inch cubes
1 small red bell pepper, finely chopped
⅓ cup finely chopped red onion
½ small jalapeño, seeds and veins removed, finely
  chopped
¼ cup fresh lime juice
2 teaspoons olive oil
2 tablespoons chopped fresh cilantro
Salt to taste

PORK CHOPS

2 teaspoons chipotle chili powder
2 teaspoons light brown sugar
2 teaspoons ground cumin
1 teaspoon garlic powder
1 teaspoon salt
4 bone-in center-cut pork chops (1 inch thick,
  about ½ pound each)
1 tablespoon canola oil

1 To make the mango salsa: In a medium bowl, combine the mango, bell pepper, onion, jalapeño, lime juice, olive oil, cilantro, and salt. Stir to coat and combine well. Let the salsa sit so the flavors can develop while you prepare the pork chops.

2 To prepare the pork chops: In a small bowl, combine the chipotle chili powder, brown sugar, cumin, garlic powder, and salt. Sprinkle this all over the pork chops, pressing the spice rub in with your fingers.

3 In a large skillet, heat the canola oil over medium-high heat. Add the chops and cook, covered and without moving them, until a dark golden crust forms on the bottom of each, 2 to 3 minutes. Flip the chops and cook, covered, for 2 to 3 minutes more. Remove the pan from the heat, flip the chops again, and let them rest, covered, in the pan for 2 minutes. Remove from the pan, tent with foil, and let rest for 3 minutes.

4 Serve the pork chops with the mango salsa alongside.

TURN DOWN THE HEAT: These pork chops have a little kick to them, thanks to the chipotle chili rub. If that's enough heat for you, go ahead and skip the jalapeño in the otherwise cooling mango salsa.

Nutritional count based on 4 servings (does not include salt to taste):
348 calories, 38g protein, 13g fat, 21g carbohydrate, 3g fiber, 697mg sodium

PORK CUBANO SANDWICHES

This is a sandwich that eats like a meal. As in a traditional Cuban sandwich, this version features two types of pork, but I've cut the fat in this decadent dish by using lean pork tenderloin for one of them. You've got to be prepared to get a little messy when eating this overstuffed sandwich. But believe me, it's well worth the cost of a few extra napkins. **SERVES 4**

½ pork tenderloin (½ pound), halved crosswise

Salt and freshly ground black pepper

1 ham steak (6 ounces), quartered

2 whole-wheat demi baguettes (about 5 ounces), sliced in half crosswise and then in half horizontally

2 tablespoons spicy brown mustard

4 slices light Swiss cheese

8 sandwich slices kosher dill pickles

1 Preheat the oven to 425°F. Line a baking sheet with aluminum foil and lightly grease it with cooking spray.

2 Season the pork all over with salt and pepper to taste. Transfer the pork to the prepared baking sheet and roast until the internal temperature reaches 145°F, about 15 minutes.

3 During the last 5 minutes of cooking time for the tenderloin, add the quartered ham steak to the baking sheet to warm through and place the baguette halves, cut sides up, directly on the oven rack to lightly brown.

4 Transfer the tenderloin to a cutting board and let it rest, tented with foil, for 5 minutes. Then cut it into 8 slices.

5 Spread 1½ teaspoons of the mustard over the cut side of each bottom piece of baguette. Top with a ham steak quarter, 2 slices of tenderloin, a slice of Swiss cheese, and 2 slices of pickle. Place the other half of the baguette on top, press the sandwich down firmly with the palm of your hand, and dig in.

Nutritional count based on 4 servings (does not include salt and black pepper to taste): 347 calories, 32g protein, 8g fat, 38g carbohydrate, 5g fiber, 914mg sodium

BOURBON-BRAISED PORK CHOPS

Even if you're not a Southerner, you are going to want to lap this Tennessee-inspired sauce right up. My goodness, this is a decadent meal if I ever tasted one. But with only 238 calories per serving, it still fits into my midweek eating plan. And for that I am so very thankful. **SERVES 4**

4 boneless pork loin chops (¾ inch thick, about 5 ounces each)
Freshly ground black pepper
2 tablespoons bourbon
1 tablespoon dark brown sugar
1 can (10½ ounces) condensed French onion soup
1 tablespoon cornstarch

1 Preheat the oven to 325°F.

2 Grease a medium ovenproof skillet with cooking spray and place it over medium heat.

3 Season the pork chops with pepper to taste, and add them to the skillet. Cook until browned on the bottom, about 5 minutes.

4 Meanwhile, in a small bowl, combine the bourbon and brown sugar and stir until smooth.

5 When the chops are brown on the bottom, turn them over and pour the bourbon mixture into the pan. Let it bubble for 5 seconds, and then pour the onion soup over the chops. Cover, transfer to the oven, and braise until cooked through, about 10 minutes.

6 Meanwhile, in a small bowl, combine the cornstarch with 1 tablespoon of water and stir until dissolved.

7 When the chops are cooked through, transfer them to a warm platter and place the skillet with the sauce over medium-high heat. Stir in the cornstarch mixture, bring to a boil, and cook, stirring, for 1 minute, until the sauce is thickened. Pour the sauce over the pork chops, and serve.

Nutritional count based on 4 servings (does not include black pepper for seasoning): 238 calories, 32g protein, 6g fat, 8g carbohydrate, 1g fiber, 607mg sodium

SPINACH AND CHEESE–STUFFED PORK CHOPS

Stuffing pork chops is a great way to jazz up a quick midweek meal, and the options are just about endless. This healthy spinach and Parmesan stuffing is right at the top of my favorites list. I love any creative way to sneak more vitamin-packed veggies into my diet, especially when it tastes this good. **SERVES 6**

6 boneless pork loin chops (¾ inch thick, about 5 ounces each)

1 package (10 ounces) frozen chopped spinach, thawed and squeezed of excess liquid

¼ cup jarred chopped pimiento

⅔ cup grated Parmesan cheese

½ teaspoon garlic powder

½ teaspoon salt, plus more to taste

¼ teaspoon freshly ground black pepper, plus more to taste

2 teaspoons olive oil

Lemon wedges, for serving

1 Preheat the oven to 350°F.

2 Pat the pork chops dry with a paper towel. Using a sharp knife, carefully cut a horizontal slit through the center of each chop to form a deep pocket.

3 In a medium bowl, combine the spinach, pimiento, Parmesan, garlic powder, salt, and pepper. Divide this stuffing among the 6 pockets. Season the chops with salt and pepper.

4 In a large, ovenproof skillet, heat the oil over medium-high heat, tilting the skillet to coat the bottom evenly. When the oil is hot, add the pork chops and cook, without moving them, until they are beginning to brown on the bottom, about 3 minutes. Flip the chops and place the skillet in the oven. Cook until the meat is no longer pink, 10 to 15 minutes. Let the chops stand for 5 minutes, then serve them with the lemon wedges.

Nutritional count based on 6 servings (does not include salt and black pepper to taste and lemon wedges for serving):
196 calories, 27g protein, 8g fat, 3g carbohydrate, 2g fiber, 452mg sodium

SWEET AND SOUR PORK MEATBALLS

These meatballs may be small in stature, but they sure do bring big flavor to the table. The sweet and sour sauce is mouthwateringly delicious and about as easy as 1-2-3 to whip up. Any sugar-free "blond" fruit marmalade or preserves (such as orange, apricot, or peach) will work in the sauce, so use the one you like the best. And don't skimp on the Tabasco—its spicy kick is a great balance to the sticky-sweet, slightly sour glaze. **SERVES 6**

MEATBALLS
2 pounds lean ground pork
6 garlic cloves, finely chopped
2 whole scallions, finely chopped
½ teaspoon Tabasco sauce
1 teaspoon chili powder
2 teaspoons salt
Freshly ground black pepper to taste

SWEET AND SOUR SAUCE
¼ cup sugar-free orange marmalade
1 teaspoon Tabasco sauce
1 large garlic clove, finely chopped
Finely grated zest and juice of ½ lime

1 Position an oven rack about 6 inches from the heat and preheat the broiler to high. Grease a rimmed baking sheet with cooking spray.

2 While the broiler is heating, prepare the meatballs: In a large bowl, combine the pork, garlic, scallions, Tabasco, chili powder, salt, and pepper. Using your hands, gently mix the ingredients together until combined. Shape the pork mixture into 1½-inch meatballs and place them on the prepared baking sheet, making sure the meatballs are at least 1 inch apart. You should wind up with between 14 and 16 meatballs.

3 Transfer the baking sheet to the oven and broil the meatballs for 5 minutes.

4 Meanwhile, make the sweet and sour sauce: In a medium bowl, whisk together the marmalade, Tabasco, garlic, lime zest, and lime juice.

5 Turn the oven temperature down to 450°F. Generously brush each meatball with the sauce, and bake for 10 minutes or until cooked through.

Nutritional count based on 6 servings (does not include black pepper to taste): 285 calories, 20g protein, 15g fat, 7g carbohydrate, 1g fiber, 887mg sodium

ALTHOUGH I WAS RAISED in a committed carnivore household, I have grown to embrace the meatless diet. At least one day out of my week, I take meat off the menu. On that day, I either toss together a vegetarian main salad from chapter 1 or I cook up one of the delicious meat-free dishes in this chapter. Most often, my meatless day is Monday. After a weekend of grilling and little indulgences here and there, it's refreshing to take a break. Vegetables and grains can be so satisfying as a meal on their own, I find I don't miss meat one bit.

It's pretty common practice down here in the South for folks to keep chicken coops in their yards and my Mama has them to this very day. There's nothing quite like a farm-fresh egg. Whether you gather them in your yard or buy them off the shelf, eggs are a great way to get protein into a meatless dinner. You can bake, poach, fry, or scramble them. There's an egg preparation out there for just about everyone. One of my personal favorites is a poached egg. Top about anything with a lovely poached egg and you've instantly fancied up the meal. WHITE BEAN AND TOMATO STEW WITH POACHED EGGS (page 109) is a colorful meal that tastes just as good as it looks. And if you don't like your eggs poached, you could always top the stew with a fried egg.

Almost any meal that can be prepared using meat can also be prepared using vegetables or grains in its place. HEARTY VEGETARIAN BURGERS (page 117) are a great example of that. These burgers are made with an aromatic mix based on bulgur and black beans. They are rich and tasty and so good that they'll make you forget all about beef burgers . . . until you get to my MEAT LOAF BURGERS (page 133) in chapter 7, that is!

And what would a meatless selection be without pasta? Whether it's baked, as in VEGETABLE BAKED ZITI (page 122), or boiled and sauced, as in CREAMY PASTA PRIMA-VERA (page 119), pasta has always been a mainstay of my diet. These days, I use whole-grain pasta more often than white-flour pasta. The complex carbs in whole-grain pastas are so much better for my body, and the nutty taste of the whole grains is a flavor I've really come to love. If it doesn't work for you, though, feel free to use regular pasta in any of the recipes that call for whole-grain.

Here's the thing: I no longer look at a meatless meal as a deprivation. In fact, I don't even find it challenging anymore. I've figured out how to create tasty, filling meals with a wide variety of ingredients that I love. The recipes in this chapter will help you find an array of meatless staples that fit your taste and lifestyle. I love food that makes me feel like I'm indulging while all the while I'm doing right by my body.

ITALIAN VEGETABLE FRITTATA

Frittatas are the type of food that fits in at any time of the day. So even though this recipe feeds six, I'll also make it when I'm cooking for one. That way I have plenty left over for breakfast the next morning and lunch the day after. And because it's just as nice at room temperature as it is hot out of the oven, I often make this frittata ahead of time. **SERVES 6**

2 teaspoons olive oil
1 small onion, thinly sliced
1 small zucchini (6 ounces), sliced into thin rounds
1 garlic clove, finely chopped
½ cup grape tomatoes (about 2 ounces), halved
2 tablespoons thinly sliced fresh basil
½ teaspoon salt
1 teaspoon freshly ground black pepper
8 large eggs
2 tablespoons skim milk
2 tablespoons grated Parmesan cheese

1 Preheat the oven to 400°F.

2 In a medium nonstick, ovenproof skillet, heat the oil over medium-high heat. Add the onion and zucchini and cook, stirring, until the zucchini is tender, 3 to 4 minutes. Add the garlic, tomatoes, basil, ¼ teaspoon of the salt, and ½ teaspoon of the pepper and cook, stirring, for 1 minute.

3 In a medium bowl, whisk together the eggs, milk, and the remaining ¼ teaspoon salt and ½ teaspoon pepper. Stir in the Parmesan. Pour the egg mixture over the vegetables and cook over medium heat until the eggs begin to set around the edges, about 2 minutes. Transfer the skillet to the oven and bake until the frittata is set all the way through, 10 to 15 minutes.

4 Remove the skillet from the oven, let the frittata cool slightly in the skillet, and then slice it into 6 equal triangles. Serve warm or at room temperature.

KEEP IT COVERED: I've got one of those old-fashioned heavy cast-iron frying pans with a wooden handle. It's my absolute favorite pan, but the handle is not ovenproof. When I need to put it in the oven, I simply cover the wooden handle with aluminum foil and it's protected from burning. This trick works with any non-ovenproof handles your pans might have.

Nutritional count based on 6 servings: 134 calories, 10g protein, 8.5g fat, 5g carbohydrate, 1g fiber, 323mg sodium

BAKED EGGS WITH TOMATOES, ONIONS, AND PEPPERS

It may sound like breakfast, but this dish is most definitely ready for prime-time dinner eating. It's downright bursting with flavor and it satisfies like you wouldn't believe. I served this meal to my buddy Sam recently, and he was bowled over. Believe me, Sam is not a light eater or easily impressed, so earning his seal of approval is something to cheer about. **SERVES 4**

2 teaspoons olive oil

½ large onion, thinly sliced

1 large red bell pepper, thinly sliced

1 small jalapeño, seeds and veins removed, thinly sliced

2 garlic cloves, thinly sliced

1 can (28 ounces) chopped tomatoes, with juices

1 teaspoon sweet paprika

½ teaspoon salt, plus more to taste

½ teaspoon freshly ground black pepper, plus more to taste

8 large eggs

¼ cup fresh basil, coarsely chopped

Grated Parmesan cheese, for serving

Crusty bread, for serving

1 Preheat the oven to 375°F.

2 In a large nonstick, ovenproof skillet, heat the oil over medium-high heat. Add the onion, bell pepper, and jalapeño and cook, stirring occasionally, until soft, about 10 minutes. Add the garlic and cook for 1 to 2 minutes. Add the tomatoes and juices, paprika, salt, and pepper. Bring to a simmer and cook until the sauce has thickened, about 8 minutes.

3 Crack the eggs, one at a time, into the sauce. Transfer the skillet to the oven and bake until the eggs are just set, 7 to 10 minutes. Season with more salt and pepper if you think it needs it. Garnish with the basil and serve with grated Parmesan and crusty bread alongside.

....

Nutritional count based on 4 servings (does not include salt and black pepper to taste and Parmesan and bread for serving): 222 calories, 15g protein, 13g fat, 14g carbohydrate, 4g fiber, 714mg sodium

WHITE BEAN AND TOMATO STEW WITH POACHED EGGS

This is the kind of hearty, stick-to-your-ribs bowl of food that will make you forget all about meat. And you won't be missing out on protein, either, I tell you! Between the beans and the eggs, this dish is protein-packed. If you're watching your carbs, feel free to skip the suggested bread for serving and dish this up with a side salad to round out the meal. **SERVES 4**

1 tablespoon olive oil
1 small onion, finely chopped
2 carrots, finely chopped
2 garlic cloves, finely chopped
1 tablespoon tomato paste
2 tablespoons white wine vinegar
1 can (28 ounces) whole tomatoes, with juices
Salt and freshly ground black pepper to taste
2 cans (15½ ounces each) cannellini beans, rinsed and drained
6 ounces thin green beans, trimmed and coarsely chopped
1 tablespoon distilled white vinegar
4 extra-large eggs
2 tablespoons chopped fresh basil
Crusty whole-wheat bread, for serving (optional)

1 In a large, deep skillet, heat the oil over medium-low heat. Add the onion and carrots and cook, stirring, until softened, 5 to 7 minutes. Add the garlic and cook for 30 seconds. Add the tomato paste and vinegar and cook for 1 minute, stirring to coat the vegetables with the paste.

2 Pour in the tomatoes and their juices, breaking up the tomatoes with the back of a spoon. Season with salt and pepper, increase the heat to medium-high, and bring to a boil. Then reduce the heat to medium and simmer for 8 minutes.

3 Add the cannellini beans and green beans, cover the pan, and cook for 5 minutes or until the green beans are just tender.

4 Meanwhile, fill a small, shallow saucepan with 2 inches of water, add the vinegar, and bring to a simmer. Break one of the eggs into a small cup and then slide the egg into the water, stirring the water very gently with a spoon. Repeat immediately with the other eggs, and cook until the whites are firm, about 3 minutes. Remove the eggs with a slotted spoon and drain them on paper towels.

5 Stir the basil into the stew, and spoon it into four individual bowls. Top each bowl with a poached egg, and serve with the bread on the side, if you like.

THE SKINNY ON BEANS: You may have noticed the skinny green beans with the pointy ends in your local supermarket. They go by the fancy name *haricots verts*, but don't be put off by that. They are snappy, flavorful little beans and I love them in a quick-cooking stew like this one. Look for them the next time you're at the market. If you don't see them, go on ahead and use regular green beans. Just be aware that you may need to cook them a touch longer, depending on how crisp you like them.

. . . .
Nutritional count based on 4 servings (does not include salt and black pepper to taste and bread for serving):
334 calories, 20g protein, 10g fat, 45g carbohydrate, 11g fiber, 407mg sodium

MUSHROOM SPINACH QUESADILLAS

I don't know many guys who aren't crazy for Tex-Mex cooking, but mention mushrooms and spinach and you might lose a fair few. So I suggest you serve this dish without forewarning on the vegetables. One bite in and the most die-hard meat lovers will be clamoring for more, I guarantee it. **SERVES 4**

2 teaspoons olive oil

1 small onion, thinly sliced

2 cups sliced button mushrooms (about 6 ounces)

¼ teaspoon crushed red pepper flakes, plus more to taste

½ teaspoon salt

¼ teaspoon freshly ground black pepper

3 cups baby spinach

8 corn tortillas (6-inch diameter)

1 cup shredded Cheddar cheese

¼ cup finely chopped fresh cilantro

½ cup jarred salsa

1 In a large skillet, heat the oil over medium heat. Add the onion and cook, stirring, until softened, about 5 minutes. Add the mushrooms and cook until they are tender, about 5 minutes. Add the red pepper flakes and cook for about 30 seconds. Season with the salt and pepper. Stir in the spinach and cook, stirring, until it has wilted, about 2 minutes. Remove the pan from the heat.

2 Position an oven rack 4 to 5 inches from the heat and preheat the broiler to medium.

3 Place the tortillas in a single layer on a baking sheet, and broil until golden, 1 to 2 minutes. Remove the baking sheet from the oven, and top half of the tortillas with the mushroom-spinach mixture, removing the other tortillas from the baking sheet. Sprinkle the tortillas on the baking sheet with the Cheddar and cilantro, and place back under the broiler. Broil until the cheese is melted, 1 to 2 minutes. Top the mushroom tortillas with the plain tortillas and serve topped with the salsa.

Nutritional count based on 4 servings: 269 calories, 12g protein, 13g fat, 28g carbohydrate, 5g fiber, 703mg sodium

EASY PARMESAN-CRUSTED ZUCCHINI

It doesn't get much easier than this delicious meat-free dish. It works with zucchini or any other summer squash you can find at the market. For a spicier take, try adding a pinch of crushed red pepper flakes to the Parmesan-panko mixture.

SERVES 4

2 zucchini (8 ounces each), sliced in half
    lengthwise
¼ teaspoon salt
¼ teaspoon freshly ground black pepper
3 tablespoons grated Parmesan cheese
2 tablespoons whole-wheat panko breadcrumbs
2 teaspoons olive oil

1 Preheat the oven to 400°F. Line a baking sheet with parchment paper.

2 Place the zucchini, cut side up, on the prepared baking sheet, and season with the salt and pepper.

3 In a small bowl, combine the Parmesan and panko. Sprinkle the Parmesan mixture over the zucchini halves and drizzle with the oil. Bake until the cheese is melted and golden and the zucchini are tender, about 20 minutes. Serve warm.

....
Nutritional count based on 4 servings:
67 calories, 3g protein, 4g fat,
6g carbohydrate, 1g fiber, 238mg sodium

CAJUN RATATOUILLE BAKE

Ratatouille is a favorite of mine, but I don't wind up fixing it very often because it takes so darn long to make. After a fair bit of trial and error, I finally figured out the answer to speedy ratatouille. First off, I slice the veggies very thin. To help out in that task, I use a mandoline—it's a great shortcut tool for creating thinly sliced, evenly sized vegetables. Second, I crank the heat up in the oven so that the veggies caramelize quickly. If I see some browning, I simply cover them with aluminum foil. I think this recipe just goes to show that where there's a will, there's a way. **SERVES 4**

2 tablespoons olive oil
2 garlic cloves, finely chopped
2 zucchini (about 1 pound), thinly sliced
1 onion, thinly sliced
1 small eggplant (about 1 pound),
    quartered lengthwise and thinly sliced
2 red bell peppers, thinly sliced
1 teaspoon Cajun spice blend
½ teaspoon salt
¼ teaspoon freshly ground black pepper
1 tablespoon chopped fresh basil
½ tablespoon chopped fresh thyme leaves
1 cup quinoa

1 Preheat the oven to 475°F.

2 In a large bowl, combine the oil, garlic, zucchini, onion, eggplant, bell peppers, Cajun spice blend, salt, and pepper. Add the basil and thyme, and toss to combine. Transfer to a 13 by 9-inch baking dish and bake until the top is golden and the vegetables are tender, about 20 minutes. If the vegetables begin to brown too much, cover the dish with aluminum foil.

3 Meanwhile, cook the quinoa: In a medium saucepan, combine the quinoa with 2 cups of water and bring to a boil. Cover, reduce the heat to low, and simmer until the quinoa is tender, about 15 minutes.

4 Fluff the quinoa with a fork and serve with the ratatouille.

IT'S NOT JUST FOR DINNER: This ratatouille makes an excellent stuffing for omelets the next morning or a great filling for wraps at lunchtime. When I use the leftovers for omelets, I like to add some canned tomatoes to the vegetables. For wraps, I throw a little soft goat cheese into the mix.

Nutritional count based on 4 servings: 302 calories, 10g protein, 10g fat, 46g carbohydrate, 11g fiber, 311mg sodium

VEGGIE MAC AND CHEESE CASSEROLE

Less cheese and a *lot* more vegetables: That's the secret behind this delicious casserole. It all works thanks to the Greek yogurt, which makes the end product unbelievably creamy and outrageously decadent, even though it's fat-free. And by using two strong-tasting cheeses like Gruyère and Parmesan, you won't even notice that the cheese is slashed by more than half the usual amount. **SERVES 6**

¼ cup fat-free Greek yogurt

1 teaspoon Dijon mustard

½ teaspoon salt

1 teaspoon freshly ground black pepper

¼ cup shredded Gruyère cheese

3 tablespoons grated Parmesan cheese

1 head cauliflower (about 1 pound),
   cut into florets, large florets halved

1 large head broccoli (about 1¾ pounds),
   cut into florets, large florets halved

1 package (13¼ ounces) whole-grain fusilli

1 cup fresh or frozen peas

2 tablespoons whole-wheat panko breadcrumbs

1 Preheat the oven to 425°F. Grease an 8-inch square baking dish with cooking spray.

2 In a small bowl, whisk together the yogurt, mustard, salt, and ½ teaspoon of the pepper. Stir in the Gruyère and Parmesan.

3 Bring a large pot of salted water to a boil over high heat. Add the cauliflower and broccoli and cook until just tender, about 5 minutes. Remove the vegetables from the water with a slotted spoon, and transfer them to a large bowl.

4 Return the water to a boil, add the pasta, and cook according to the package directions. About a minute before the pasta is finished cooking, add the peas and cook until heated through. Drain the peas and pasta, reserving 1 cup of the pasta cooking water, and transfer them to the bowl containing the cauliflower and broccoli.

5 Add the yogurt mixture and ½ cup of the pasta cooking water to the pasta and veggie mixture, and stir until the cheese is melted and the mixture is well combined; add more pasta water if it seems a little dry. Transfer the mixture to the prepared baking dish, and sprinkle with the panko and the remaining ½ teaspoon pepper. Bake until the cheese is bubbly, about 10 minutes.

Nutritional count based on 6 servings: 341 calories, 18g protein, 4g fat, 65g carbohydrate, 12g fiber, 353mg sodium

THREE-BEAN AND KALE CHILI

Beans, kale, and mushrooms always work nicely together. So I thought, why not in a chili? This is a mild, earthy-tasting chili, but if you prefer a bit of heat in your Tex-Mex, you can easily amp up the spice by keeping the seeds in your chopped jalapeño. Just be sure to have a little bread on hand to soak up the burn and then crack open a (light) beer to cool things right down. **SERVES 6**

2 tablespoons vegetable oil

½ pound button mushrooms, stems trimmed, chopped

1 onion, chopped

1 can (15½ ounces) small white beans, rinsed and drained

1 can (15½ ounces) black beans, rinsed and drained

1 can (15½ ounces) red kidney beans, rinsed and drained

3 garlic cloves, chopped

1 jalapeño, seeds and veins removed, chopped

2 cups packed chopped kale

1 can (14½ ounces) diced tomatoes, with juices

1 cup low-sodium chicken broth

2 tablespoons chili powder

Salt and freshly ground black pepper

1. In a large Dutch oven, heat the oil over medium-high heat. Add the mushrooms and onion and cook, stirring frequently, until the onion has softened and the mushrooms are browned, 8 to 10 minutes.

2. Add the white beans, black beans, kidney beans, garlic, jalapeño, kale, tomatoes and juices, broth, chili powder, and salt and pepper to taste. Stir well to combine, and bring to a boil. Cover, reduce the heat to medium, and simmer for 10 minutes. Adjust the seasonings to taste, and serve.

Nutritional count based on 6 servings (does not include salt and black pepper to taste): 211 calories, 12g protein, 6g fat, 35g carbohydrate, 11g fiber, 722mg sodium

HEARTY VEGETARIAN BURGERS

I'm never one to knock a good old-fashioned beef burger. But I truly love these veggie burgers and more often than you'd think, I find myself craving these beany burgers over their meaty cousins. They are filled with awesome heat and spice that set your mouth watering. And the creamy texture of the beans matches up so nicely with the slightly crunchy bulgur. Feel free to fiddle with the toppings based on what you like on your regular burgers. **SERVES 5**

1 cup fine bulgur
½ teaspoon salt, plus more to taste
1 cup boiling water
⅓ cup light mayonnaise
2 teaspoons Sriracha or other chili sauce
1 can (15½ ounces) black beans,
   rinsed and drained
1 large egg, lightly beaten
½ teaspoon freshly ground black pepper
½ tablespoon chili powder
½ tablespoon ground cumin
Pinch of cayenne pepper
¼ cup finely chopped fresh cilantro or basil
1 garlic clove, smashed
5 light multigrain English muffin halves, toasted
1 teaspoon olive oil
½ small avocado, pitted, peeled, and thinly sliced
Tomato slices, for serving
Boston lettuce leaves, for serving

1 In a medium heatproof bowl, combine the bulgur, salt, and boiling water. Cover with a towel and let sit for 20 minutes.

2 Meanwhile, stir together the mayonnaise and Sriracha in a small bowl.

3 In a food processor, combine the bulgur with the beans, egg, pepper, chili powder, cumin, cayenne, cilantro or basil, garlic, and more salt to taste. Pulse until thoroughly combined. Form into 5 equal patties (about ¼ pound each), making sure the patties are flat and wider than the English muffins.

4 In a medium nonstick skillet, heat ½ teaspoon of the oil over high heat. Working in batches, and adding the remaining ½ teaspoon oil as needed, cook the burgers for 4 to 5 minutes, or until crispy and golden brown on the bottom. Flip the burgers and cook for an additional 4 to 5 minutes.

5 Place each burger on a toasted muffin half, spread with the chili mayo, and then top with the avocado. Serve topped with tomato slices and lettuce leaves.

BIG BULGUR: Bulgur is a whole-wheat grain that is popular in the Middle East but very easy to find in supermarkets in the States. It's known for its mild, nutty flavor and wide range of health benefits. It's high in fiber, low in fat, and chock-full of minerals. Plus, I love that it can be jazzed up with pretty much any herb, vegetable, or dressing.

Nutritional count based on 5 servings (does not include tomato and lettuce for serving): 345 calories, 14g protein, 11g fat, 57g carbohydrate, 16g fiber, 881mg sodium

BAKED BBQ TOFU

I was skeptical about tofu for years. I just could not understand what people saw in it. It wasn't until I tasted it tossed into a full-flavored sauce that I began to see how great it really could be. When I make this dish, I use my favorite barbecue sauce because the tofu soaks up every bit of its flavor. It's outrageously delicious. And baking tofu is genius. It comes out crispy on the outside and pillowy soft on the inside. Give it a go and see if it doesn't win you over, too. **SERVES 4**

1 block (16 ounces) extra-firm tofu
¼ cup jarred barbecue sauce
1 teaspoon fresh lemon juice
½ teaspoon Dijon mustard
¼ teaspoon hot sauce
1 tablespoon finely chopped scallions, white and light green parts only

1 Preheat the oven to 400°F.

2 Wrap the tofu between layers of paper towels and place on a plate. Cover with another plate and weight it down with a heavy can. Set aside to drain for about 5 minutes. Then discard the liquid and paper towels, and cut the tofu into 1-inch cubes.

3 Place the tofu on a rimmed baking sheet, and coat the cubes lightly with cooking spray. Bake, flipping the cubes halfway through the cooking time, until golden brown and crisp, about 20 minutes.

4 In a medium bowl, whisk together the barbecue sauce, lemon juice, mustard, and hot sauce. Add the tofu and toss to coat. Sprinkle with the scallions and serve warm.

Nutritional count based on 4 servings: 127 calories, 11g protein, 7g fat, 8g carbohydrate, 1g fiber, 199mg sodium

CREAMY PASTA PRIMAVERA

While this pasta is creamy all right, it doesn't contain a lick of cream. Greek yogurt stands in for the traditional cream sauce here, and I believe it does a darn fine job. I like to call this "decadent health food." If you'd like to add even more of a healthy nutritional kick to this meal, toss in some baby spinach just at the end, stirring it through the hot pasta until it wilts. Or if you prefer a non-creamy version, skip the yogurt. **SERVES 4**

1 bunch asparagus (about 1 pound),
   woody ends snapped off, cut into 1-inch pieces
½ pound whole-grain spiral pasta
1 cup fresh or frozen peas
1 teaspoon olive oil
1 onion, finely chopped
1 garlic clove, finely chopped
¼ teaspoon crushed red pepper flakes
1 cup grape tomatoes (about ¼ pound),
   halved lengthwise
3 tablespoons fat-free Greek yogurt
3 tablespoons thinly sliced fresh basil
Juice of ½ lemon
3 tablespoons grated Parmesan cheese
½ teaspoon salt
½ teaspoon freshly ground black pepper

1 Bring a large pot of salted water to a boil over high heat. Fill a medium bowl with ice water and set it aside.

2 When the water is boiling, add the asparagus and cook until just tender, about 2 minutes. Remove the asparagus with a slotted spoon and submerge it in the ice water for a minute or two to cool down. Then, using a slotted spoon, transfer the asparagus to a large bowl.

3 Return the water in the pot to a boil. Add the pasta and cook according to the package directions. About a minute before the pasta is finished cooking, add the peas and cook until they are heated through. Drain the pasta and peas, and add them to the bowl containing the asparagus.

4 In a large skillet, heat the oil over medium-high heat. Add the onion and cook until tender, about 5 minutes. Add the garlic and red pepper flakes and cook until the garlic is fragrant, about 1 minute. Add the tomatoes and stir for 1 minute, until they are heated through.

5 Add the onion-tomato mixture to the pasta mixture, and stir in the yogurt, half of the basil, the lemon juice, Parmesan, salt, and pepper. Toss to combine, sprinkle with the remaining basil, and serve.

Nutritional count based on 4 servings: 303 calories, 16g protein, 3g fat, 58g carbohydrate, 10g fiber, 372mg sodium

SUNNY-SIDE-UP PORTOBELLO BURGERS

The Worcestershire sauce in this vegetarian burger gives the meaty portobello mushrooms a real authentic beefy flavor. Even though these sandwiches are a far healthier option than your traditional beef burger, they certainly do deliver on the taste front. And the fried egg topping is like the icing on the cake. I like my yolks runny, but if you prefer yours hard-cooked, feel free to cook the eggs a couple minutes longer. **SERVES 4**

8 portobello mushrooms
1 tablespoon Worcestershire sauce
¼ teaspoon salt
½ teaspoon freshly ground black pepper
4 whole-wheat English muffins, split and toasted
1 teaspoon olive oil
4 large eggs
Tomato slices, for serving
Boston lettuce leaves, for serving
Ketchup, for serving

1 Position an oven rack 5 inches from the heat and preheat the broiler to high.

2 Using a damp kitchen towel, clean the mushrooms. Remove the stems, and use a spoon to scrape out and discard the dark gills. Place the mushrooms, flat side up, on a rimmed baking sheet and brush them with the Worcestershire. Place the baking sheet in the oven and broil for 2 minutes. Flip the mushrooms and broil for 2 minutes more, or until they are tender and browning. Remove from the oven and sprinkle with the salt and pepper. Place 2 mushroom caps on each of 4 toasted muffin bottoms and cover with aluminum foil to keep warm.

3 In a medium nonstick skillet, heat ½ teaspoon of the oil over high heat. Crack 2 eggs into the skillet. Cook for 1 minute or until the whites are set and the bottom is beginning to brown, and then flip and cook for 30 seconds more, or longer if you don't like your yolks runny. Remove them from the skillet and repeat with the remaining ½ teaspoon oil and the remaining eggs. Transfer the cooked eggs to the mushroom burgers and serve topped with the tomato, lettuce, ketchup, and the English muffin tops.

Nutritional count based on 4 servings (does not include tomato, lettuce, and ketchup for serving):
263 calories, 16g protein, 8g fat, 37g carbohydrate, 7g fiber, 579mg sodium

VEGETABLE BAKED ZITI

I love feeding a crowd, even if it does take a little more effort in the up-front preparation. Fact is, I love food for a crowd, even if I don't have a whole mess of people to feed, because I know I'll have lots of leftovers for the busier days in my week. When it comes to feeding an army, there's nothing much better than baked ziti. This meal is so good, your Italian *mamma* will think you slaved over the stove for hours on end. And you'll know that you didn't! **SERVES 8**

1 package (13¼ ounces) whole-grain ziti

1 pound zucchini, quartered lengthwise, then cut crosswise into ½-inch chunks

½ pound button mushrooms, stems trimmed, quartered

¼ teaspoon Paula Deen's House Seasoning (page 49)

1 jar (24 ounces) light, no-sugar-added pasta sauce

1 cup (8 ounces) low-fat cream cheese (Neufchâtel)

1 package (10 ounces) frozen spinach, thawed and squeezed of excess liquid

Crushed red pepper flakes to taste

½ cup shredded part-skim mozzarella cheese

¾ cup grated Parmesan cheese

1 Position oven racks in the two highest positions in your oven. Preheat the oven to 450°F. Grease two rimmed baking sheets with cooking spray. Grease a 13 by 9-inch baking dish with cooking spray.

2 In a large pot of boiling salted water, cook the pasta according to the package directions. Drain the pasta, reserving ¼ cup of the pasta water.

3 Meanwhile, arrange the zucchini, in one layer, on one of the prepared baking sheets. Arrange the mushrooms on the second prepared baking sheet. Grease the vegetables lightly with cooking spray and sprinkle with the House Seasoning. Roast until the mushrooms are brown, about 8 minutes, and

the zucchini is just tender, about 2 minutes more, switching the position of the baking sheets after 5 minutes. Reduce the oven temperature to 400°F and reposition a rack in the center of the oven.

4 While the pasta is cooking and the vegetables are roasting, prepare the sauce: In a medium saucepan over medium heat, combine the jarred pasta sauce, cream cheese, and spinach and cook, stirring, until the cream cheese is melted. Season with the red pepper flakes.

5 In a large bowl, combine the drained pasta, roasted vegetables, sauce, and reserved pasta cooking water. Scrape into the prepared baking dish, and top with the mozzarella and Parmesan cheeses. Bake until the cheeses are melted and bubbly, about 10 minutes.

GRILLING LEFTOVERS: When I grill vegetables on the weekend, I tend to grill in large quantities so I'll have leftovers to use throughout the week in sandwiches, salads, and whatever else I can think of. This baked ziti is a great place to use leftover grilled veggies, making this one-dish meal even quicker from start to finish.

Nutritional count based on 8 servings (does not include crushed red pepper flakes to taste):
339 calories, 20g protein, 10g fat, 47g carbohydrate, 7g fiber, 873mg sodium

I HAVE ALWAYS LOVED BEING OUTDOORS. Any chance I get to cook outside, you can be sure I'll take it. And since I'm fortunate enough to live in a beautiful climate like Savannah's, that's possible just about all through the year. The way I see it, preparing dinner on the grill just doesn't feel like work. Getting home after a busy day and going out to the backyard to throw dinner on reads less like a chore and more like quality relaxation time.

As in many other families, when I was a kid it was my dad who did most of the grilling. While Jamie and I tossed the ball around, climbed trees, and ran about the yard like wild boys, he'd be out there grilling with a nice cold drink in hand, tongs at the ready, and a truly happy smile on his face. As I got older, he taught me everything I know about cooking outside, from barbecue basics right on through to advanced grilling techniques.

Let's face it—you don't have to be a trained chef to master the barbecue. For that reason alone, it's tailor-made for quick midweek cooking. There aren't many dishes that are faster and easier to put together than BUTTERMILK AND HERB–MARINATED GRILLED CHICKEN THIGHS (page 134). It takes less than ten minutes to cook them to perfection!

There's plenty of debate as to whether charcoal or gas grilling is better. That's a debate I choose to stay out of, and for an obvious reason: I use both! I see why the purists tout the virtues of charcoal grilling. There's nothing quite like the natural smoky flavor from an open fire, especially for red meats like my CHIMICHURRI STEAKS (page 135). But from a time perspective, you can't beat the ease of firing up a gas grill with the push of a button. I admit, if I didn't have the gas option, I'd do far less grilling during the week. In general, I save the charcoal for the weekends.

Outdoor cooking is not just for meat, though. Vegetables taste so much better when they're cooked over the high heat of the barbecue. GRILLED CORN WITH PIMIENTO CHEESE (page 143) is a great example. While some people wrap their corn in foil before placing it on the barbecue, I like to place mine directly on the heat, where it blackens and chars to sweet perfection. If you've never tried bread baked on the grill, you're in for a real treat with my GRILLED WHOLE-WHEAT FLATBREADS (page 140). All they need is a simple smattering of olive oil and salt to make them shine, but they reach new heights of tastiness with toppings like ricotta, sautéed spinach, or sliced tomatoes.

Barbecues have a funny way of inviting people over. Just a whiff of that smoky smell in the air tells the neighbors that something good is going on. My friends always show up with beer in hand or a side salad for the table. And lucky man that I am, I have a wife who shares that social gene and is always happy to set another place.

SALMON STEAKS WITH OLIVE AND PEPPER RELISH

If you're a meat lover who wants to give fish a try, salmon steaks are the cut for you. Even my most committed carnivore friends are psyched when they see I'm grilling these up. They are rich, meaty, good for you, and boast an incredible buttery taste. I love to top them with a zingy salty relish like this one. I think it brings out all the best features in the salmon steak. **SERVES 4**

¼ cup pitted kalamata olives, finely chopped
2 jarred or fresh roasted red bell peppers, finely chopped
2 tablespoons finely chopped fresh basil
3 teaspoons olive oil
2 teaspoons red wine vinegar
½ teaspoon freshly ground black pepper
4 skin-on salmon steaks (6 ounces each)
½ teaspoon salt
Juice of 1 lemon

1 In a large bowl, toss together the olives, roasted bell peppers, basil, 1 teaspoon of the oil, the vinegar, and ¼ teaspoon of the black pepper.

2 Generously grease a grill grate with cooking spray, and preheat the grill to medium-high heat.

3 Season the salmon steaks with the salt and the remaining ¼ teaspoon pepper, and drizzle with the remaining 2 teaspoons oil. Grill the salmon, without turning it, for 7 minutes, until the center is warmed through and opaque. Transfer the salmon steaks to plates, sprinkle with the lemon juice, and serve with the olive-pepper relish.

WORRY-FREE GRILLING: I know a lot of people get worried about grilling fish. But really, there's nothing to be nervous about. Just follow these few simple rules and you will be a pro in no time: First off, make sure your grill grate is very well oiled (notice the recipe says "generously grease"). Then, get your grill good and hot. Last, leave the fish alone to do its cooking. Don't go trying to flip it before it's done. You'll know it's ready to move when you can easily slip your spatula under the fish and lift it off. And if all else fails, you can always wrap your fish in aluminum foil, as I do with my *Ham-Stuffed Trout* (page 128). Happy grilling!

Nutritional count based on 4 servings: 328 calories, 36g protein, 19g fat, 2g carbohydrate, 0g fiber, 442mg sodium

HAM-STUFFED TROUT

Claudia introduced me to this Spanish-style trout dish that she grew up eating in Venezuela. Traditionally it's made with a Spanish ham called Serrano. I loved it so much, I just had to go ahead and put the old Bobby spin on it. I chop up ham steak and mix it with parsley and almonds to create a salty, herby stuffing for the fish. I like to wrap the fish in aluminum foil to make it super easy to grill. Then I lift the packages off the barbecue and bring them right to the table as is. These trout taste great with simple grilled asparagus and brown or white rice. **SERVES 4**

½ cup finely chopped ham steak
   (from ½ ham steak slice)
⅓ cup chopped fresh parsley
2 tablespoons slivered almonds, toasted
1 lemon
4 boned whole trout (about ¾ pound each)
Salt and freshly ground black pepper to taste
2 tablespoons unsalted butter, cut into cubes

1 In a medium bowl, stir together the ham, parsley, and almonds to combine well.

2 Trim the ends off the lemon and cut it in half. Slice one half of the lemon into 4 rounds, and then slice each round into halves, making 8 half-moons. Cut the other half of the lemon into wedges and set them aside.

3 Cut 8 rectangles of aluminum foil large enough to wrap each trout. Stack the foil sheets to create 4 double-layered rectangles. Grease the top layer of each foil rectangle with cooking spray.

4 Rinse the fish and pat them dry with paper towels. Place on the prepared foil sheets. Season the fish inside and out with salt and pepper. Scatter the butter cubes evenly inside the trout cavities. Divide the ham mixture among the trout cavities, and lay 2 half-moon lemon slices in each. Fold the trout over to enclose the filling. Fold the foil over the fish to completely enclose them, sealing the edges of the foil.

5 Preheat the grill to medium heat.

6 Lay the fish packets on the grill, cover the grill, and cook for about 5 minutes. Then flip the packets, re-cover the grill, and cook for another 4 minutes, or until the trout flakes easily when tested with a fork. Serve with the lemon wedges.

HEADS UP: Three-quarters of a pound may seem like a lot of fish for one person to eat, but keep in mind that that's the weight of the whole trout, with the head and tail on. If you're a little squeamish about seeing the whole fish on your plate, go on ahead and have your fishmonger remove the heads before you take the trout home.

Nutritional count based on 4 servings (does not include salt and black pepper to taste): 317 calories, 38g protein, 17g fat, 4g carbohydrate, 3g fiber, 154mg sodium

GRILLED CHICKEN CAESAR SALAD

A good chicken Caesar salad is something I have a hard time turning down. But when it comes to the Caesar salad served in most restaurants, I do try to have the self-control to give it a pass—most of them contain a crazy amount of fat and calories. So I like to make my own version on my grill at home. It's a classic but it never gets old. **SERVES 4**

1 tablespoon white wine vinegar
1 tablespoon fresh lemon juice,
    plus ½ lemon for squeezing
1 tablespoon Dijon mustard
2 tablespoons light mayonnaise
1 tablespoon olive oil
½ teaspoon garlic powder
½ teaspoon salt
3 boneless, skinless chicken breasts
    (6 ounces each)
2 romaine lettuce hearts, trimmed and
    coarsely chopped
⅔ cup store-bought Caesar salad croutons
⅓ cup coarsely grated Parmesan cheese
Freshly ground black pepper to taste

1 In a small bowl, whisk together the vinegar, lemon juice, mustard, mayonnaise, oil, garlic powder, and salt. Place 1 tablespoon of this dressing in a medium bowl, and add the chicken to that bowl. Coat the chicken thoroughly with the marinade and let it sit while you preheat the grill.

2 Grease a grill grate with cooking spray, and preheat the grill to medium heat.

3 Grill the chicken for about 6 minutes per side. Transfer it to a cutting board, tent it with aluminum foil, and let it rest for 5 minutes.

4 Meanwhile, in a large bowl, toss the lettuce, croutons, Parmesan, and reserved dressing.

5 Cut the chicken into thick slices and add them to the salad. Squeeze the lemon half over the top and sprinkle with black pepper. Toss once more, and serve.

SUBS AND SWAPS: As they do in restaurants, I often sub out the classic choice of chicken in this dish. Caesar salad is equally delicious with grilled shrimp, salmon, or steak.

Nutritional count based on 4 servings (does not include black pepper to taste): 283 calories, 35g protein, 11g fat, 9g carbohydrate, 3g fiber, 685mg sodium

GRILLED CUMIN CHICKEN AND POTATO SALAD

This is a complete meal that's best enjoyed outdoors. The light and creamy yogurt dressing makes for a cooling potato salad that is the perfect complement to the smoky chicken and peppers. Feel free to have a heavy hand with the fresh herbs sprinkled on top. And if you can't decide between parsley and basil, why, I suggest you use them both! **SERVES 4**

4 boneless, skinless chicken breasts
  (6 ounces each)
1 teaspoon ground cumin
Juice of 1 lemon
1 teaspoon salt, plus more to taste
¾ teaspoon freshly ground black pepper
1½ tablespoons olive oil
1 red bell pepper, quartered
1 yellow bell pepper, quartered
16 baby red potatoes (about 8 ounces), halved
⅓ cup fat-free Greek yogurt
1 garlic clove, finely chopped
2 whole scallions, thinly sliced
Chopped fresh parsley or fresh basil, for garnish

1 Grease a grill grate with cooking spray, and preheat the grill to medium heat.

2 While the grill is preheating, combine the chicken, cumin, lemon juice, ¾ teaspoon of the salt, ½ teaspoon of the pepper, and 1 tablespoon of the oil in a resealable plastic bag and shake the bag to combine.

3 Remove the chicken from the bag, letting any excess marinade drip off. Grill the chicken for about 6 minutes per side and the bell peppers until tender and lightly charred, about 3 minutes per side. Transfer the chicken and peppers to a cutting board, tent with aluminum foil, and let rest for 10 minutes.

4 Meanwhile, fill a medium pot with cold water. Add the potatoes and remaining ¼ teaspoon salt and bring to a boil. Cook for 8 minutes or until fork-tender. Drain and set aside.

5 In a medium bowl, combine the remaining ½ tablespoon oil, the yogurt, garlic, scallions, and remaining ¼ teaspoon black pepper. Add the potatoes, toss to combine, and then add salt to taste.

6 Slice the chicken and serve it with the grilled peppers and the potato salad. Garnish everything with chopped parsley or basil.

Nutritional count based on 4 servings (does not include salt to taste or parsley/basil for garnish):
315 calories, 42g protein, 8g fat, 18g carbohydrate, 3g fiber, 715mg sodium

BUTTERMILK AND HERB–MARINATED GRILLED CHICKEN THIGHS

When I'm stuck in a barbecue sauce rut, I like to mix things up and make this light and simple buttermilk and herb marinade. If I've got a little time on my hands, I let the chicken sit in the marinade for 30 minutes or so, but even without the marinating time, the bright herby flavor shines right through. **SERVES 4**

4 boneless, skinless chicken thighs
   (¼ pound each), trimmed of excess fat
½ cup low-fat buttermilk
1 garlic clove, finely chopped
2 tablespoons finely chopped fresh basil,
   plus more for garnish
1 teaspoon finely chopped fresh thyme
½ teaspoon salt
½ teaspoon freshly ground black pepper
1 lemon

1 Grease a grill grate with cooking spray, and preheat the grill to medium heat.

2 In a medium bowl or large resealable plastic bag, combine the chicken thighs, buttermilk, garlic, basil, thyme, salt, and pepper. Finely grate the lemon zest and add it to the bowl or bag. Cut the lemon into wedges and reserve for serving. If you are using a bag, give the bag a good shake to coat the chicken all over with the marinade.

3 Remove the chicken from the bowl or bag, letting any excess marinade drip off, and grill for 4 minutes per side, or until it is cooked through and the internal temperature registers 165°F on an instant-read thermometer. Transfer the chicken to a cutting board, cover it with aluminum foil, and let it rest for 10 minutes.

4 Serve the chicken garnished with more chopped basil and with the reserved lemon wedges alongside.

....
Nutritional count based on 4 servings (does not include basil for garnish):
158 calories, 24g protein, 5g fat, 5g carbohydrate, 1g fiber, 414mg sodium

CALIFORNIA TURKEY BURGERS

How many times have you had a boring, dry-tasting turkey burger? Well, it's too many times for my liking. And while I love a good beef burger, with bun and typical fixings, one serving can approach a whopping 500 calories! I've found that the key to a tasty, juicy turkey burger is lots of seasoning in the patty mix and a couple teaspoons of oil both in the mix and brushed on the outside of the patties. That's all it takes to achieve a scrumptious, tender burger without too many extra calories. I like to go a little crazy with the toppings to really jazz up my sandwich, and this recipe is no exception. **SERVES 4**

1 pound lean ground turkey

1 garlic clove, finely chopped

3 tablespoons finely chopped fresh parsley

½ teaspoon hot sauce, or more to taste

½ teaspoon salt

1 teaspoon freshly ground black pepper

4 teaspoons canola oil

1 small red onion, sliced into thick rounds

2 whole-wheat hamburger buns, split open and toasted

½ avocado, pitted, peeled, and sliced lengthwise into 8 equal slices

½ cup alfalfa sprouts

1 Grease a grill grate with cooking spray, and preheat the grill to medium-high heat.

2 In a large bowl, combine the turkey, garlic, parsley, hot sauce, salt, and pepper. Pour in 2 teaspoons of the oil and combine. Using your hands, form into 4 equal patties.

3 Brush both sides of the burgers with 1 teaspoon of the remaining oil and place them on the grill. Cook until evenly browned and cooked through, 4 to 6 minutes per side.

4 Meanwhile, brush the onion rounds with the remaining 1 teaspoon oil, and place them on the grill. Grill until browned on one side, about 2 minutes; then flip and grill until browned on the second side, about 2 minutes more.

5 Serve the turkey burgers open-faced on the toasted buns, with the grilled onion slices, avocado slices, and sprouts piled on top.

Nutritional count based on 4 servings: 307 calories, 23g protein, 18g fat, 15g carbohydrate, 5g fiber, 519mg sodium

MEAT LOAF BURGERS

Since the days of my Grandmama Paul, my family has had a bit of a love affair with meat loaf. We just keep thinking up new ways to change it up. A meat loaf burger seemed so obvious after we thought of it, we couldn't believe it hadn't come to mind before! This is a summer staple for us. Sitting next to my *German Potato Salad with Turkey Bacon* (page 161), it's like heaven on a plate. **SERVES 4**

1 teaspoon olive oil

1 small onion, finely chopped

1 celery stalk, finely chopped

1 garlic clove, finely chopped

1 pound 95%-lean ground beef

¼ cup dried whole-wheat breadcrumbs

1 medium egg, lightly beaten

1 teaspoon dried thyme

¾ teaspoon salt

½ teaspoon freshly ground black pepper

¼ cup low-sodium ketchup

1 tablespoon spicy brown mustard

2 teaspoons Worcestershire sauce

4 whole-wheat hamburger buns

Lettuce, for serving

Sliced tomato, for serving

1 Heat the oil in a nonstick skillet over medium heat. Add the onion and celery and cook until soft, about 8 minutes. Stir in the garlic and cook for 1 minute. Set aside to cool for 5 minutes.

2 In a large bowl, using your hands, gently mix the cooled vegetables with the beef, breadcrumbs, egg, thyme, salt, and pepper until just combined. Divide the mixture into 4 equal patties.

3 Lightly grease a grill grate with cooking spray, and preheat the grill to medium-high heat.

4 Meanwhile, in a small bowl, whisk together the ketchup, mustard, and Worcestershire.

5 Cook the burgers until they are about halfway through their cooking time, about 3 minutes per side if you like them medium-rare. Then brush the tops of the burgers generously with the ketchup glaze, flip them, and cook until caramelized on the bottom, about 2 minutes. Repeat with the other side. Remove from the grill and brush both sides of each burger with more glaze. Sandwich the burgers between the buns, and serve topped with lettuce and tomato.

RAINY DAYS: Even I have to admit that some days just aren't for grilling. If that's the case and you still want to make these delicious burgers, you can always cook them under the broiler. Simply preheat the broiler to high and set a wire rack over a foil-lined baking sheet. Then cook and glaze the burgers just as you would on the grill.

Nutritional count based on 4 servings (does not include lettuce and tomato for serving): 349 calories, 31g protein, 11g fat, 31g carbohydrate, 3g fiber, 854mg sodium

CHIMICHURRI STEAKS

Chimichurri is a mouthwateringly delicious sauce made from fresh herbs, garlic, vinegar, and oil. It originated in Argentina, where they use it on their meat of choice: beef. I use it here on skirt steak, which is one of my favorite cuts to grill and also one of the leanest. To enjoy them at their succulent best, I recommend cooking these steaks only to medium-rare. **SERVES 6**

¼ cup fresh parsley leaves

3 tablespoons olive oil

1 tablespoon red wine vinegar

1 tablespoon fresh oregano leaves
   (or substitute 1 teaspoon dried oregano)

3 garlic cloves, coarsely chopped

Pinch of crushed red pepper flakes

Salt and freshly ground black pepper

1½ pounds skirt steak, cut into 6 equal pieces

1 In a blender or small food processor, combine the parsley, oil, vinegar, oregano, garlic, and red pepper flakes, and blend to a coarse puree. Season to taste with salt and pepper. Rub half of the marinade on the steaks and place the remainder in a small bowl.

2 Grease a grill grate with cooking spray, and preheat the grill to medium-high heat (the steaks will marinate while the grill heats).

3 Grill the steaks for 3 to 5 minutes per side or until the internal temperature reaches 120°F on an instant-read thermometer for medium-rare (or a few minutes longer, until the temperature reaches 130°F, for medium). Let the meat rest for about 5 minutes before serving it with the reserved bowl of chimichurri on the side.

Nutritional count based on 6 servings (does not include salt and black pepper to taste): 195 calories, 26g protein, 10g fat, 1g carbohydrate, 0g fiber, 64mg sodium

CUMIN LAMB KEBABS WITH YOGURT-DILL SAUCE

It's been known for years that the Mediterranean diet is one of the healthiest there is. What a bonus that it's also one of the tastiest! It's basically the food of Greece, southern Italy, and Spain. Common ingredients include olive oil, fresh vegetables and fruit, yogurt, fish, and lamb. If you're not especially familiar with lamb, this recipe is a great way to be introduced to it. These richly flavored skewers are juicy, tangy, and tender. **SERVES 4**

1 tablespoon olive oil

2 teaspoons finely chopped garlic

1 teaspoon ground cumin

1 teaspoon honey

½ teaspoon salt, plus more to taste for the yogurt sauce

Freshly ground black pepper

1 pound boneless leg of lamb, trimmed of excess fat and cut into 1-inch cubes

¾ cup low-fat Greek yogurt

2 tablespoons chopped fresh dill

2 teaspoons fresh lemon juice

4 metal or wooden skewers (if using wooden skewers, soak them in water for 20 minutes)

1 In a large bowl, whisk together the oil, 1½ teaspoons of the garlic, the cumin, honey, salt, and pepper to taste. Add the lamb and toss to coat it evenly.

2 Grease a grill grate with cooking spray, and preheat the grill to high heat.

3 Meanwhile, in a small serving bowl, combine the yogurt, dill, lemon juice, remaining ½ teaspoon garlic, and salt to taste.

4 Thread the lamb cubes onto the skewers, making sure to leave some space between the pieces so that they cook evenly. Grill, turning the skewers once, until done to your liking, about 3 minutes per side for medium-rare. Serve with the yogurt sauce alongside.

Nutritional count based on 4 servings (does not include salt and black pepper to taste): 230 calories, 26g protein, 11g fat, 7g carbohydrate, 0g fiber, 415mg sodium

GRILLED PORK TENDERLOIN SALAD

This is the type of dish I like during the hot summer months. You know the days when you just can't think of turning on the oven and you don't feel like weighing yourself down with anything too heavy? Those are the days I created this pork salad for. It's light yet satisfying and you won't overheat when you're prepping it up. **SERVES 6**

2 teaspoons red wine vinegar
1 teaspoon finely chopped shallot
Pinch of salt, plus more to taste
1 pork tenderloin (1½ pounds), cut into 6 pieces
3 tablespoons apricot preserves
1 tablespoon Dijon mustard
Freshly ground black pepper to taste
One bag (5 ounces) baby arugula
1 pint grape tomatoes, halved
2 tablespoons olive oil

1 Lightly grease a grill grate with cooking spray and preheat the grill to medium-high heat.

2 In a small bowl, combine the vinegar, shallot, and the pinch of salt; let the shallot pickle while you prepare the pork. In a second small bowl, combine the preserves and mustard; set aside.

3 Place the pork pieces between two sheets of plastic wrap and, using a meat pounder or the bottom of a heavy skillet, pound the pork to ⅛-inch thickness.

4 Season the pork lightly with salt and pepper, and grill on one side for 1½ minutes, until grill marks appear. Flip the pork and brush the cooked sides with half of the apricot glaze. Continue to grill until cooked through, about another 1½ minutes, and then turn and brush the second side with the glaze. Arrange the pork on a large serving platter.

5 In a large bowl, combine the arugula and tomatoes. Whisk the olive oil into the shallot mixture and toss into the salad. Serve the salad piled on top of the pork.

Nutritional count based on 6 servings (does not include salt and black pepper to taste): 207 calories, 24g protein, 8g fat, 10g carbohydrate, 1g fiber, 405mg sodium

GRILLED WHOLE-WHEAT FLATBREADS

Grilled bread is definitely one of the finer things in life. And you don't need much to make it taste so good—just a bit of olive oil and salt does the trick most of the time. But when you're after something a little special, fresh herbs and garlic really turn up the volume. I use fresh rosemary in this particular recipe—its bold flavor stands up well to grilling. See ideas for toppings following the recipe.

SERVES 4

All-purpose flour, for dusting
1 ball (8 ounces) prepared whole-wheat
    pizza dough
1 teaspoon finely chopped fresh rosemary
¼ teaspoon salt
1 teaspoon olive oil
1 large garlic clove, halved lengthwise

1 Grease a grill grate with cooking spray, and preheat the grill to medium-high heat.

2 Place a sheet of parchment paper on your counter, dust it with flour, and roll out the pizza dough to form an 8- to 10-inch-long oval about ¼ inch thick. Let the dough rest for 5 minutes.

3 In a small bowl, combine the rosemary and salt. Rub each side of the dough with ½ teaspoon of the oil, and sprinkle each side with the rosemary salt.

4 Grill the flatbread for 2 to 3 minutes, until crisp and lightly charred on the bottom. Flip the flatbread and continue grilling for an additional 2 to 3 minutes, until the dough is cooked through. Transfer to a cutting board and rub each side with the cut sides of the garlic. Cut into pieces and serve.

TOP IT UP: It's super easy to turn this grilled flatbread into a barbecue pizza. Here are a couple great ideas to start you off, but use your imagination to find your favorite combination.

1. After flipping the flatbread, dollop it with fat-free ricotta and ¼ cup shaved Parmesan. Close the grill lid and cook until the cheese has slightly melted. Serve topped with baby arugula and a squeeze of lemon juice.

2. After flipping the flatbread, sprinkle with ⅓ cup shredded low-fat mozzarella. Close the grill lid and cook until the cheese has melted. Serve topped with ½ cup halved cherry tomatoes and a sprinkling of chopped fresh basil.

Nutritional count based on 4 servings (does not include flour for dusting):
153 calories, 4g protein, 5g fat, 25g carbohydrate, 2g fiber, 546mg sodium

GRILLED CORN WITH PIMIENTO CHEESE

This great twist on corn on the cob manages to combine corn with one of my favorite Southern specialties—pimiento cheese. What an easy way to dress up this summer staple! By the end of August, I'm always searching for new and interesting ways to serve corn. This little beauty has become one of my favorite new riffs on an oldie but goodie. **SERVES 8 / MAKES 1 CUP PIMIENTO CHEESE**

2 tablespoons low-fat cream cheese (Neufchâtel), at room temperature
1 cup shredded low-fat Cheddar cheese
3 tablespoons light mayonnaise
1½ tablespoons jarred chopped pimientos, mashed with a fork
¼ teaspoon Worcestershire sauce
Pinch of onion powder
Freshly ground black pepper to taste
8 ears corn, shucked
Lime wedges, for serving

1 Grease a grill grate with cooking spray, and preheat the grill to medium-high heat.

2 Using a handheld mixer, beat the cream cheese until fluffy. Beat in the Cheddar, mayonnaise, pimientos, Worcestershire, onion powder, and pepper until well combined.

3 Place the ears of corn on the grill and cook, covered, turning them occasionally, until tender, 10 to 15 minutes.

4 Spread 2 tablespoons of the pimiento cheese over each ear of corn, and serve with the lime wedges.

Nutritional count based on 8 servings (does not include black pepper to taste and lime wedges for serving):
173 calories, 8g protein, 4g fat, 31g carbohydrate, 4g fiber, 155mg sodium

A GREAT SIDE DISH REALLY COMPLETES A MEAL. A beautifully cooked steak or a fresh piece of fish is nothing if it doesn't come with the right sidekick. There are certain pairings that I think go especially well together. If it's beef or lamb I'm preparing, I like to have hearty green vegetables like asparagus or Brussels sprouts, or sweet roasted veggies such as carrots and parsnips. When I'm cooking chicken on the barbecue, I can't help but stick it next to corn, either on the cob or in a nice light salad. And a fish dinner feels complete with a delicate vegetable companion like steamed green beans.

While I love that I can get my hands on just about any veggie at any time of the year, most often I try to prepare vegetables that are in season. During their peak growing season, vegetables taste so much better and are less expensive to boot. Claudia and I love spending our Saturday mornings at our local farmers' market, picking out the produce we'll use throughout the week.

When it's cold outside, I usually crave hearty, starchy vegetables like parsnips and potatoes. Throughout January and February, my pantry is well stocked with both sweet and regular potatoes. SWEET AND SPICY BAKED SWEET POTATOES (page 160) is a winter staple that fills the house with the warming smell of cinnamon. Earthy mushrooms are great in winter stews and soups, or prepared on their own, as in BROILED HERBED MUSHROOMS (page 154), and then served next to a fine steak.

Once April hits, I tend to start eating a little lighter. With the warmer weather, I begin to think about being outdoors and getting myself ready for summer. I can't get enough of sweet snow peas and crisp asparagus. Asian-style ASPARAGUS AND SNOW PEA STIR-FRY (page 159) really highlights the great flavor and tender texture of these two vegetables during the spring months.

Of course, summer is all about zucchini, tomatoes, and corn. TOMATO AND ZUC-CHINI WITH FETA (page 146) is a celebration of that harvest. I cook these vegetables simply so that their natural sweetness can shine through. And zucchini and corn get baked into ZUCCHINI CORN FRITTERS (page 156), always popular with friends who stop by for lunch or dinner.

Whether my veggies are fresh, frozen, or canned, I strive to eat as many as I can. If I'm short on the fresh variety, a quick stir-fry or simple soup can be based on frozen mixed vegetables or peas, and that meal is just as good for me as the one made with fresh vegetables. I know that a good, healthy, satisfying meal can't be far away when I've got vegetables to prepare it with.

TOMATO AND ZUCCHINI WITH FETA

Although summer veggies are the stars of this dish, I make it year-round. In the summer, because the vegetables are at their peak tenderness, I tend to cook it a bit less, maybe shaving off a minute or two from the total cooking time. In the winter, I like to cook the zucchini and tomatoes down just a little bit longer. The white balsamic really comes in handy to sweeten up the dish when I'm using off-season tomatoes. However, if you can't find white balsamic, you can use a fruity cider vinegar instead. This quick vegetable sauté works great as a side to the *Roasted Lemon-Olive Chicken Thighs* (page 69) or simply tossed through chunky pasta for a one-dish meal. **SERVES 4**

1 tablespoon olive oil
2 small zucchini (6 ounces each), coarsely chopped
1 tablespoon white balsamic vinegar or cider vinegar
¼ teaspoon salt
2 garlic cloves, thinly sliced
1 pint grape tomatoes, halved
2 tablespoons chopped fresh oregano
1 tablespoon fresh lemon juice, plus more to taste
⅓ cup crumbled feta cheese
Freshly ground black pepper to taste

1 In a large skillet, heat the oil over medium heat. Add the zucchini and cook, stirring occasionally, until it is lightly browned and almost tender, about 4 minutes.

2 Add the vinegar, salt, garlic, and tomatoes and cook, stirring occasionally, until the tomatoes begin to soften and release their juices but are still largely intact, about 5 minutes.

3 Stir in the oregano and cook for 1 minute. Remove from the heat.

4 Just before serving, stir in the lemon juice. Give it a taste and add more lemon juice if you think it needs it. Sprinkle the feta and black pepper over the top.

IT'S A WRAP: If you manage to have leftovers of this dish, it tastes delicious in a wrap the next day. When I need to take my lunch with me, I fold cooked veggie leftovers into whole-grain tortillas and then wrap them up in portable aluminum foil packages. It's nice to know that when you can't make it back home for a homemade lunch, you can bring that homemade lunch right along with you.

Nutritional analysis based on 4 servings (does not include lemon juice and black pepper to taste):
94 calories, 4g protein, 6g fat, 7g carbohydrate, 2g fiber, 296mg sodium

ROASTED BRUSSELS SPROUTS

My Mama tends to lightly boil her sprouts and then pan-fry them with lots of salty bacon. They are delicious. But my preferred cooking method for these little green beauties is roasting. I love the way a high oven temperature brings out their natural sweetness. After I pull them out of the oven, I toss them in lots of freshly grated Parmesan for a lip-smacking salty finish. See photograph page 149.

SERVES 4

1 pound Brussels sprouts,
    trimmed and halved lengthwise
1 tablespoon plus 1 teaspoon olive oil
1 teaspoon finely grated lemon zest
Salt and freshly ground black pepper
¼ cup grated Parmesan cheese

1 Preheat the oven to 400°F.

2 In a large bowl, toss the Brussels sprouts with the oil and lemon zest, and season with salt and pepper to taste. (Be careful not to add too much salt, as the Parmesan will add some saltiness.) Transfer the sprouts to a rimmed baking sheet and roast until just tender, about 20 minutes, giving the pan a good shake halfway through the cooking time so that the sprouts brown evenly.

3 Return the Brussels sprouts to the large bowl, toss with the Parmesan cheese, and serve.

Nutritional count based on 4 servings (does not include salt and black pepper to taste): 115 calories, 6g protein, 7g fat, 10g carbohydrate, 4g fiber, 124mg sodium

MAPLE-GLAZED CARROTS

This recipe actually originated with my nephew Jack. He loves his carrots extra sweet, so we started roasting them with maple syrup. He couldn't get enough of them and neither could the adults! With the addition of a pinch of cayenne and a grinding of black pepper, this dish has thoroughly grown up. **SERVES 6**

2 tablespoons pure maple syrup
½ cup low-sodium chicken broth
Pinch of cayenne pepper
2 bunches small carrots (about 14 carrots)
½ teaspoon salt, plus more to taste
½ teaspoon freshly ground black pepper
1 tablespoon unsalted butter,
    cut into small pieces
Chopped fresh parsley, for garnish

1 Preheat the oven to 425°F.

2 In a small saucepan, stir together the syrup, broth, and cayenne. Cook over high heat until the mixture is reduced by half, about 10 minutes.

3 Meanwhile, rinse and peel the carrots. If the carrots still have their greens, trim off all but a ½-inch top. Leave carrots whole if they are very thin. Otherwise halve or quarter them lengthwise.

4 Place the carrots in a single layer on a rimmed baking sheet, and drizzle the syrup mixture over them. Sprinkle with the salt and pepper, and dot with the butter. Roast for 12 to 15 minutes, shaking the pan halfway through, until the carrots are fork-tender and beginning to brown. Transfer to a serving platter, add more salt if you like, and serve garnished with parsley.

Nutritional count based on 6 servings (does not include parsley for garnish): 84 calories, 1g protein, 2g fat, 16g carbohydrate, 3g fiber, 474mg sodium

BRAISED RED CABBAGE WITH BACON AND DRIED CRANBERRIES

If you asked me, I'd say that the smoky bacon is the star of this warm cabbage dish. If you asked Claudia, she'd cast her vote for the sweet and tangy dried cranberries. Whichever ingredient you think is the star, there's no denying that they work perfectly together. And what a sight this makes on the table! The red cabbage turns a deep, purple color that jazzes up any meal. This side tastes fantastic served next to *Spinach and Cheese–Stuffed Pork Chops* (page 100). See photograph page 149. **SERVES 6**

1 tablespoon canola oil
1 shallot, chopped
2 strips bacon, chopped
1 head red cabbage (1½ pounds), cored and shredded
⅓ cup dried cranberries
Salt and freshly ground black pepper

1 In a large Dutch oven, heat the oil over medium heat. Add the shallot and bacon and cook, stirring frequently, until the shallot turns lightly golden, about 3 minutes. Add the cabbage and toss to coat all over. Cover the pot and cook, stirring occasionally, until the cabbage has wilted, 10 to 15 minutes.

2 Stir in the cranberries, cover again, and cook for 2 minutes. Season to taste with salt and pepper.

Nutritional count based on 6 servings (does not include salt and black pepper to taste): 120 calories, 3g protein, 7g fat, 14g carbohydrate, 3g fiber, 108mg sodium

ROASTED PARSNIPS

As these parsnips roast, their sugars concentrate to intensify their awesome sweetness. To balance that sweet note, I coat them with cumin, cayenne, and thyme. I like to serve this winter vegetable next to a juicy piece of beef or lamb.

SERVES 4

8 small parsnips (about 1¼ pounds), peeled and cut into ¼-inch pieces

2 tablespoons olive oil

½ teaspoon ground cumin

¼ teaspoon cayenne pepper

2 teaspoons finely chopped fresh thyme

1 teaspoon salt

½ teaspoon freshly ground black pepper

1 **Preheat the oven to 400°F.**

2 **Put the parsnips in a 13 by 9-inch baking dish, and drizzle with the oil. Sprinkle with the cumin, cayenne, thyme, salt, and pepper, and toss to coat well. Cover the dish with aluminum foil and roast until the parsnips are tender, about 15 minutes. Serve warm.**

Nutritional count based on 4 servings: 167 calories, 2g protein, 7g fat, 26g carbohydrate, 7g fiber, 596mg sodium

BIG OL' POT OF GREENS

I remember the good old days when my Mama used to cook up a big pot of greens for Sunday family dinner. Those greens would be on the stove from morning 'til afternoon. And they'd be simmering away with a ham hock and a stick of butter! Well, I have found a healthy way to cook my greens and still get that smoky taste, silky texture, and divine pot liquor. And because mine take less than 30 minutes from start to finish, I don't have to wait until Sunday to enjoy them. **SERVES 4**

1 teaspoon olive oil

1 strip turkey bacon, thinly sliced crosswise

3 garlic cloves, thinly sliced

3 large bunches collard greens, Swiss chard, or mustard greens (about 1½ pounds), stems removed and leaves sliced

Pinch of crushed red pepper flakes

½ teaspoon salt, plus more to taste

½ teaspoon freshly ground black pepper

Hot sauce, for serving

1 In a large pot, cook the oil and bacon over medium-high heat until the bacon is beginning to crisp, about 3 minutes. Add the garlic and cook until it is fragrant but not browned, about 30 seconds.

2 Add the greens, red pepper flakes, salt, and pepper. Stir to combine, and cook for 1 minute. And ¼ cup of water, cover the pot, and reduce the heat to medium-low. Cook for 10 to 12 minutes, until the greens are tender and the liquid has reduced.

3 Add more salt to taste, and serve with the hot sauce for passing.

·····································

Nutritional count based on 4 servings (does not include salt to taste and hot sauce for serving):
85 calories, 7g protein, 3g fat, 9g carbohydrate, 6g fiber, 493mg sodium

BROILED HERBED MUSHROOMS

These mushrooms are my healthier take on the classic steakhouse side. Instead of sautéing them in heaps of butter like they do in restaurants, I caramelize them on high heat under the broiler, using just 1 tablespoon of heart-healthy olive oil. The result is a side dish with a mere 48 calories per serving! I serve them with *Mustard-Rubbed Flank Steak* (page 86) and a fresh green salad. It's a simple meal that looks and tastes so good that it's more than worthy of company on a Saturday night, but easy enough for any given Monday. **SERVES 4**

1 pound button mushrooms, stems trimmed

1 tablespoon olive oil

2 teaspoons Worcestershire sauce

½ teaspoon freshly ground black pepper

Juice of ¼ lemon

¼ teaspoon salt, plus more to taste

1 tablespoon chopped fresh parsley

1 tablespoon chopped fresh dill

1 Position an oven rack about 10 inches from the heat and preheat the broiler to high.

2 Cut the small mushrooms in half and the large mushrooms into quarters. In a medium bowl, toss the mushrooms with the oil, Worcestershire, and pepper. Spread the mushrooms on a rimmed baking sheet and broil for 8 to 10 minutes, until tender and browned.

3 Remove the mushrooms from the oven and transfer them to a serving platter. Sprinkle the lemon juice and salt over the mushrooms, adding more salt to taste. Scatter the parsley and dill over the top, and serve.

EATING IN: This recipe is a perfect example of how easy it is to take restaurant food and make it healthier at home. Eating out is a treat, but for everyday cooking, I like to re-create restaurant dishes in my own kitchen, minus the excess fat, calories, and sodium. And when I'm the one dishing out the servings, I'm also in charge of portion size, which is a major factor in keeping my weight under control.

Nutritional count based on 4 servings (does not include salt to taste):
48 calories, 2g protein, 4g fat, 3g carbohydrate, 1g fiber, 183mg sodium

HOT ROASTED GREEN BEANS WITH SWEET CHILI

This addictive side boasts the sweet and spicy Asian flavors I love so much. I use Sriracha chili sauce for the spice, which can be found in the international section of most supermarkets. If you can't get your hands on it, though, feel free to use another hot sauce to your liking. **SERVES 6**

1 pound green beans, trimmed
2 teaspoons olive oil
1 garlic clove, finely chopped
2 teaspoons honey
1 to 2 teaspoons Sriracha or other hot sauce
Juice of ½ lemon
Pinch of salt, or more to taste

SPICY SRIRACHA: Sriracha is a thick hot sauce that is named after a town in Thailand. It's made from chile peppers, garlic, vinegar, sugar, and salt and it's absolutely delicious. It's become so popular over the past couple of years that you can now find it on the tables of some diners across the country!

Nutritional count based on 6 servings (does not include salt to taste):
46 calories, 1g protein, 2g fat, 8g carbohydrate, 3g fiber, 41mg sodium

1 Preheat the oven to 425°F.

2 On a rimmed baking sheet, toss the green beans with the oil. Roast for 10 minutes, tossing halfway through, until the beans are tender and beginning to brown.

3 Meanwhile, in a large bowl, combine the garlic, honey, Sriracha, and lemon juice.

4 Remove the green beans from the oven and immediately transfer them to the bowl with the Sriracha mixture. Add the salt and toss to combine. Serve hot.

ZUCCHINI CORN FRITTERS

I recently found out that these fritters are a sneaky way to get kids to eat their vegetables. I brought them out one night when my family was over. After running back into the kitchen for a serving utensil, I came back to a half-empty platter. Turned out my nephews had gobbled them up without even knowing they were stuffing themselves full of zucchini and corn! **SERVES 4 TO 6**

2 zucchini (1 pound), coarsely grated

1½ cups fresh or frozen corn kernels, thawed if frozen

½ cup dried whole-wheat breadcrumbs

⅓ cup finely chopped onion

1 large egg, lightly beaten

½ teaspoon dried oregano

Salt and freshly ground black pepper to taste

2 tablespoons vegetable oil

1 Place the grated zucchini in a colander set over the sink and, using your hands, squeeze out as much liquid as you can. Then wrap the zucchini in a clean kitchen towel and squeeze again. Place the zucchini in a medium bowl and stir in the corn, breadcrumbs, onion, egg, oregano, and salt and pepper.

2 In a large skillet, heat the oil over medium heat until hot but not smoking. One at a time, scoop up ¼ cup of the zucchini mixture, pour it into the skillet, and press on it to form a 2½-inch patty. Cook the patties, in batches, until browned on both sides, about 3 minutes per side. Transfer to a paper-towel-lined platter to drain. (You should have about 15 fritters.) Serve immediately.

FLIP TIP: These fritters have to be turned carefully to avoid splitting them apart. I reckon the two-spatula method is most effective: To turn a fritter, use the first spatula to flip it onto the back of the second spatula, and then let the fritter slide back into the pan. By gently sliding them, you will avoid the dangerous leap back into the pan, keeping them firmly intact.

 Nutritional count per fritter (does not include salt and black pepper to taste):
56 calories, 2g protein, 3g fat, 7g carbohydrate, 1g fiber, 35mg sodium

LEMONY CABBAGE SLAW

This is not the slaw of my childhood picnics, which generally arrived on my plate drowning in a sea of mayonnaise. This grown-up version is lightly dressed, fresh, and crunchy. That's the way I prefer my veggies these days. The dressing is just subtle enough to give the cabbage, carrots, and radishes room to sit up and be noticed. See photograph page 157. **SERVES 8**

Grated zest and juice of 1 lemon

¼ cup light mayonnaise

1 teaspoon Dijon mustard

½ teaspoon salt, plus more to taste

½ teaspoon freshly ground black pepper, plus more to taste

1 small head green cabbage (about 1½ pounds), cored and finely shredded

2 large carrots, shredded

1 small bunch radishes (about 5 ounces), thinly sliced

½ small red onion, thinly sliced into half-moons

½ cup coarsely chopped fresh parsley, plus more for serving

In a large bowl, whisk together the lemon zest, lemon juice, mayonnaise, mustard, salt, and pepper. Add the cabbage, carrots, radishes, onion, and parsley. Toss to coat, and adjust the salt and pepper to taste. Serve garnished with more parsley.

KEEP IT CRISP: Unlike classic coleslaw, this slaw has a little crunch. I still prepare it ahead of time, but I don't dress it until about 30 minutes before I'm going to serve it.

Nutritional count based on 8 servings (does not include salt and black pepper to taste and parsley for serving):
61 calories, 2g protein, 3g fat, 9g carbohydrate, 3g fiber, 241mg sodium

ASPARAGUS AND SNOW PEA STIR-FRY

When springtime rolls around, I reckon I make this stir-fry about once a week. That's the time asparagus and snow peas are at their peak and are nearly everywhere you look. Truth be told, I've cooked this in the dead of winter using frozen vegetables—it's that good! Try this alongside other Asian-inspired dishes like *Stir-Fried Chicken with Green Beans and Cashews* (page 76) or *Shrimp Coconut Curry* (page 46). **SERVES 4**

1 teaspoon toasted sesame oil,
  plus more for drizzling (optional)
½-inch piece fresh ginger, peeled and finely
  chopped
1 garlic clove, finely chopped
⅛ teaspoon crushed red pepper flakes, plus more
  for serving (optional)
3 cups snow peas (about 5 ounces), trimmed
1 bunch asparagus (about 1 pound), woody ends
  snapped off, sliced on the diagonal into 1-inch
  pieces
2 teaspoons low-sodium soy sauce
White sesame seeds, for serving

1 In a medium skillet, heat the oil over high heat. Add the ginger, garlic, and red pepper flakes and cook, stirring, until fragrant but not burning, 30 seconds.

2 Add the snow peas, asparagus, and soy sauce. Cook, stirring occasionally, until the vegetables are tender and beginning to brown, about 5 minutes. (If the bottom of the pan begins to burn, just splash a tablespoon of water on the vegetables.) Transfer to a serving plate and serve sprinkled with sesame seeds, and more red pepper flakes and sesame oil if you like.

Nutritional count based on 4 servings (does not include white sesame seeds, crushed red pepper flakes, and sesame oil for serving):
64 calories, 4g protein, 1g fat, 10g carbohydrate, 4g fiber, 93mg sodium

SWEET AND SPICY BAKED SWEET POTATOES

My Mama loves baked sweet potatoes, especially when they're all dressed up with honey, cinnamon, and cayenne pepper. So when I know she's coming round for a visit, I like to whip up this side for her. It never fails to put a smile on her face. And as you probably know, my Mama's smile can light up a room. **SERVES 6**

2 large sweet potatoes (about 2 pounds), peeled and cut into 1-inch pieces

1 tablespoon olive oil

½ tablespoon honey

¼ teaspoon ground cinnamon

½ teaspoon dried thyme

Pinch of cayenne pepper

½ teaspoon salt, plus more to taste

1 Preheat the oven to 400°F.

2 In a large bowl, toss the sweet potatoes with the oil, honey, cinnamon, thyme, cayenne, and salt. Place the sweet potatoes in a single layer on a rimmed baking sheet. Bake until the potatoes are fork-tender and golden brown, about 25 minutes. Add more salt to taste, and serve.

. . . .
Nutritional count based on 6 servings (does not include salt to taste):
71 calories, 1g protein, 2g fat, 12g carbohydrate, 1g fiber, 200mg sodium

GERMAN POTATO SALAD WITH TURKEY BACON

There are so many variations of potato salad out there, but my absolute favorite is the German style. I love how the tangy mustard and vinegar cut the heaviness of the potatoes. And the bacon adds the salty note I crave. To keep the fat count down, I use lower-calorie turkey bacon. **SERVES 8**

2 pounds medium red new potatoes
4 strips turkey bacon, finely chopped
½ small red onion, finely chopped
2 teaspoons whole-grain mustard
¼ cup red wine vinegar
Juice of 1 lemon
3 tablespoons olive oil
½ teaspoon salt
¼ teaspoon freshly ground black pepper
1 tablespoon finely chopped fresh dill

1 Bring a large pot of salted water to a boil over high heat. Add the potatoes and cook until they are just tender and the tip of a knife easily pierces the flesh, 20 to 25 minutes.

2 Meanwhile, heat a medium skillet over medium-high heat. Grease the skillet with cooking spray and add the bacon. Cook, stirring, until browned, about 7 minutes. Transfer to a paper-towel-lined plate to cool.

3 Drain the potatoes well, place a towel over them, and let them steam for 5 minutes.

4 As soon as you can handle them, cut the potatoes in half (or quarters if they are larger) and place them in a medium bowl.

5 In a large bowl, whisk together the onion, mustard, vinegar, lemon juice, oil, salt, and pepper. Add the potatoes and bacon to the bowl, and toss to coat. Serve warm or at room temperature, sprinkling with the dill just before serving.

....
Nutritional count based on 8 servings: 182 calories, 6g protein, 9g fat, 19g carbohydrate, 2g fiber, 487mg sodium

I'M SURE I'M NOT THE ONLY ONE who grew up on white rice, white-flour pasta, and, since I'm from the South, grits. Those were the grains in my household, and boy oh boy did I love them. Thing is, though, as I grew into adulthood those grains began to turn on me. My body started to tell me that they didn't quite love me back. By the time I reached thirty, I knew I had to make a change. Luckily for me, my epiphany came right around the time some healthier options started popping up on supermarket shelves.

Today I'm all about whole-grain pastas, rice, and couscous. And I've discovered how versatile and tasty more exotic whole grains like bulgur and quinoa are. If you haven't tasted quinoa yet, try the QUINOA, BLACK BEAN, AND CORN SALAD (page 172) and I guarantee it will hook you, too. This superfood comes from South America, just like my beautiful wife, Claudia. She was introduced to quinoa as a child and immediately fell for its nutty flavor. Quinoa, which is actually the seed of the plant, is prepared like other grains such as barley and rice. It's the perfect food to fuel you up for a workout because it's jam-packed with protein rather than starch. Since my wife and I are pretty obsessed with fitness, you can bet it pops up on our menu quite a bit.

For a quick-cooking grain, it doesn't get any speedier than whole-wheat couscous. Just bring a pot of water to a boil, pour in the couscous, cover the pot, take it off the heat, and in five minutes the couscous is ready to serve. It can be used as a stuffing, as in COUSCOUS-STUFFED PEPPERS (page 166), or cooked with veggies and other flavorings and then served as a salad, as in SPICY CARROT AND COUSCOUS SALAD (page 170).

Cooking brown rice can be a tricky proposition when you're short on time. Fortunately, there are some really great instant brown rice products out there, including microwave packets. I use them all the time on weeknights.

And just because I am a tried-and-true Southern boy who loves his corn grits, I couldn't help but include a polenta recipe in here. CREAMY SPINACH POLENTA (page 177) tastes so decadent, you're going to think I'm pulling the wool over your eyes when I tell you it boasts a mere 253 calories per serving. But scout's honor, it's the whole delicious truth.

BULGUR PILAF WITH CHICKPEAS, ALMONDS, AND RAISINS

I usually make up a big batch of this pilaf so that I have plenty to add to salads and wraps throughout the week. Because it's best at room temperature, all I need to do is pull it out of the fridge to take the chill off while I put together the rest of my meal. It will stay fresh in the refrigerator for several days. If it makes it that long, that is. **SERVES 6**

1 tablespoon olive oil
1 onion, thinly sliced
1 cup fine bulgur
1 can (15½ ounces) chickpeas,
   rinsed and drained
1¾ cups low-sodium chicken broth
⅓ cup raisins
1 tablespoon unsalted butter
¼ cup smoked almonds, coarsely chopped
Salt and freshly ground black pepper

1 In a large skillet, heat the oil over medium heat. Add the onion and cook, stirring occasionally, until browned, about 10 minutes.

2 Meanwhile, in a medium saucepan, combine the bulgur, chickpeas, broth, raisins, and butter. Bring to a boil, stir, cover, and reduce the heat to low. Cook until the liquid has been absorbed, about 10 minutes.

3 Stir the browned onions and the almonds into the bulgur, and season with salt and pepper to taste. Transfer to a serving bowl and let cool for 5 to 10 minutes before serving.

Nutritional count based on 6 servings (does not include salt and black pepper to taste): 282 calories, 9g protein, 8g fat, 46g carbohydrate, 9g fiber, 269mg sodium

BULGUR TABBOULEH

Be sure you don't skimp on the fresh herbs in this light summer side because they bring huge flavor to the table. And lots of lemon keeps the dish bright and refreshing—just what I'm looking for after a long hot day. **SERVES 4**

1 cup fine bulgur

½ teaspoon salt, plus more to taste

Juice of 1 lemon, plus more to taste

1 tablespoon olive oil

½ teaspoon freshly ground black pepper

2 cups cherry or grape tomatoes (about ½ pound), halved

1 seedless English cucumber (about ½ pound), quartered and cut into ½-inch pieces

¼ cup finely chopped fresh parsley

¼ cup finely chopped fresh mint

1 In a medium saucepan, combine the bulgur, salt, and 1 cup of water. Bring to a boil over medium-high heat and cook for 5 minutes. Then remove from the heat and let it sit, covered, for 10 minutes or until the liquid has been absorbed.

2 Scrape the bulgur into a large bowl. Gently fold in the lemon juice, oil, pepper, tomatoes, cucumber, parsley, and mint. Adjust the salt to taste, and add more lemon juice if you think it needs it.

Nutritional count based on 4 servings (does not include salt and lemon juice to taste): 177 calories, 6g protein, 4g fat, 33g carbohydrate, 8g fiber, 306mg sodium

COUSCOUS-STUFFED PEPPERS

If you can boil water, you can make couscous. I love this grain because it cooks in just 5 minutes and works with just about any style of food. Here, it takes the place of rice in a flavorful stuffing mix for bell peppers. Sometimes I throw some cheese in the mix if I'm in the mood. I think feta is best, but Cheddar, pepper Jack, or Gruyère would also suit this simple dish. You can serve this as a satisfying side dish for four, or it makes a very light meal for two. **SERVES 4**

2 very small zucchini (about 5 ounces each), chopped

4 large red bell peppers

1½ cups low-sodium vegetable broth

1 cup whole-wheat couscous

3 ounces cooked ham, chopped (about 1 cup chopped)

2 teaspoons olive oil

1 tablespoon finely chopped fresh basil

1 tablespoon finely chopped fresh mint

½ teaspoon salt

1 Preheat the oven to 400°F. Grease a 13 by 9-inch baking dish with cooking spray.

2 Scatter the zucchini across half of the baking dish. Slice the stems and the top ½ inch off the bell peppers, and scoop out and discard the seeds and membranes. Add the peppers, cut-side up, to the baking dish, nestled next to the zucchini. The peppers should fit snugly into the dish without covering the zucchini. Bake until the peppers are beginning to soften and the zucchini is tender, about 10 minutes.

3 While the peppers are baking, prepare the couscous: In a medium saucepan over medium-high heat, bring the broth to a boil. Add the couscous, cover the pan with a tight-fitting lid, and remove from the heat. Let it steam, covered, for 5 minutes.

4 Use a fork to fluff the couscous. Stir in the roasted zucchini, the ham, oil, basil, mint, and salt. Fill the peppers with the couscous-vegetable mixture. Return the baking dish to the oven, and bake for 15 minutes longer. Serve immediately.

HERB GARDEN: I have to admit that I don't have the greenest of thumbs. I leave that talent to my Mama. However, even I can manage to grow fresh herbs in my garden. They grow like weeds and need very little tending. And that's a very good thing because I use tons and tons of them in my dishes. Herbs are a great way to add flavor without adding fat or calories.

Nutritional count based on 4 servings: 272 calories, 12g protein, 5g fat, 48g carbohydrate, 6g fiber, 670mg sodium

WHOLE-WHEAT SESAME NOODLES

I love bringing these noodles to summer barbecues, especially when Brooke and Jamie are hosting. My big brother can't get enough of Asian flavors and he just about flips when I arrive with this dish in my hands. It's nutty, refreshing, just a little bit spicy, and it pairs up nicely with almost anything you can throw on the grill. Or make this the centerpiece of a completely vegetarian meal by adding a side of *Hot Roasted Green Beans with Sweet Chili* (page 155). **SERVES 6**

½ pound whole-grain spaghetti

2 carrots, grated

3 whole scallions, thinly sliced

1 garlic clove, finely chopped

2 tablespoons low-sodium soy sauce

1 tablespoon rice vinegar

1 teaspoon toasted sesame oil

2 tablespoons peanut or vegetable oil

1¼-inch piece fresh ginger, peeled and grated

¼ teaspoon crushed red pepper flakes, or more to taste

White sesame seeds, for garnish

1 In a large pot of boiling salted water, cook the pasta according to the package directions. Drain the pasta well, rinse it under cold water, and transfer it to a large bowl. Add the carrots and scallions.

2 In a small bowl, combine the garlic, soy sauce, vinegar, sesame oil, peanut or vegetable oil, ginger, and red pepper flakes. Pour this over the noodles and toss to combine. Serve garnished with white sesame seeds.

COOL CUSTOMER: These noodles are great at room temperature but even better after they've been chilled in the fridge. If you've got the time, prep them in the morning and stick them in the fridge for the day. They are a cooling treat on a warm day.

Nutritional count based on 6 servings (does not include red pepper flakes to taste and sesame seeds for serving):
192 calories, 5g protein, 6g fat, 30g carbohydrate, 4g fiber, 247mg sodium

SPICY CARROT AND COUSCOUS SALAD

Grated onion and carrot add flavor and volume to this colorful couscous dish. Grating the veggies, which can be done by hand with a box grater or in a food processor, is a clever trick that makes quick work of preparing this salad. I like to serve this Moroccan-inspired side with another great Middle Eastern dish, *Cumin Lamb Kebabs with Yogurt-Dill Sauce* (page 136). **SERVES 4**

1 teaspoon olive oil

1 small onion, grated

1 garlic clove, finely chopped

1 teaspoon ground cumin

½ teaspoon salt, plus more to taste

1 cup whole-wheat couscous

2 large carrots, grated

Juice of 1 lime

½ teaspoon freshly ground black pepper

¼ cup chopped fresh mint or fresh parsley

Hot sauce, for serving

1 In a small saucepan, combine the oil, onion, garlic, cumin, and salt. Cook over high heat, stirring occasionally, until the onion softens but does not brown, about 2 minutes. Add the couscous and cook for 2 minutes, stirring to toast it all over. Add the carrots and 1 cup of water, bring to a boil, and then remove from the heat. Cover the pan with a kitchen towel and then with the lid, and let it sit for 10 minutes or until all the liquid has been absorbed.

2 Scrape the couscous into a serving bowl, fluff it with a fork, and add the lime juice, pepper, and mint or parsley. Toss to combine, and add more salt to taste. Serve with hot sauce for passing.

Nutritional count based on 4 servings (does not include salt to taste and hot sauce for serving):
201 calories, 6g protein, 2g fat, 40g carbohydrate, 4g fiber, 322mg sodium

WHOLE-WHEAT ITALIAN PASTA SALAD

I used to make this bold-flavored pasta salad to bring along to cookouts and picnics. I quickly realized, however, that it also made a great midweek side. It's so quick to put together, and I almost always have the ingredients in my pantry and fridge. Any leftovers are delicious for lunch the next day. **SERVES 4**

½ pound whole-grain corkscrew-shaped pasta, such as fusilli

1 shallot, finely chopped

1 garlic clove, finely chopped

3 tablespoons bottled light Italian dressing

¼ teaspoon salt

15 pitted kalamata olives, thinly sliced

½ cup sliced jarred roasted red bell pepper

1 teaspoon freshly ground black pepper

2 tablespoons finely chopped fresh basil

1 In a large pot of boiling salted water, cook the pasta according to the package directions. Drain it well, and set aside to cool slightly.

2 In a medium bowl, whisk together the shallot, garlic, dressing, and salt. Add the cooled pasta, the olives, and the bell pepper. Season with the black pepper and stir to combine. Sprinkle with the basil, and serve warm or at room temperature.

Nutritional count based on 4 servings: 245 calories, 9g protein, 4g fat, 47g carbohydrate, 6g fiber, 453mg sodium

QUINOA, BLACK BEAN, AND CORN SALAD

This chapter would not be complete without a quinoa salad. It simply doesn't get much better than this superfood, which is an awesome source of protein and fiber. The carbohydrates you'll find in quinoa have a low glycemic index, which will help you if your goal is to lose weight. And to top all that off, quinoa has a nutty flavor that is out of this world. **SERVES 8**

1 cup quinoa, rinsed and drained

1 teaspoon salt

4 teaspoons olive oil

1 cup fresh or frozen corn kernels,
    thawed if frozen

½ teaspoon crushed red pepper flakes

1 can (15½ ounces) no-salt-added black beans,
    rinsed and drained

Grated zest and juice of ½ lime

½ small red onion, finely chopped

½ teaspoon freshly ground black pepper

2 tablespoons finely chopped fresh basil

1 In a medium saucepan, stir together the quinoa, 2 cups of water, and ¼ teaspoon of the salt. Bring to a boil over medium-high heat, reduce the heat to medium-low, cover the pan, and simmer until the liquid has been absorbed, 12 to 15 minutes. Set the pan aside, covered, for 5 minutes. Then fluff the quinoa with a fork and transfer it to a large bowl.

2 In a large skillet, heat 2 teaspoons of the oil over medium-high heat. Add the corn, red pepper flakes, and ¼ teaspoon of the salt and cook, stirring occasionally, until the corn is tender and starting to brown, 4 to 5 minutes. Add the corn to the bowl containing the quinoa, and return the skillet to the heat.

3 Reduce the heat to medium and add the remaining 2 teaspoons oil and the black beans to the skillet. Stir in the lime zest and cook until the beans are heated through, 2 to 3 minutes.

4 Add the beans to the bowl containing the quinoa. Add the onion, lime juice, remaining ½ teaspoon salt, pepper, and basil and stir just to combine. Serve warm or at room temperature.

SMOKY CORN: If you've got the time, I highly recommend grilling ears of corn for this salad. The smoke from the charred corn kernels adds tons of awesome flavor.

Nutritional count based on 8 servings: 154 calories, 7g protein, 2g fat, 27g carbohydrate, 5g fiber, 293mg sodium

BROWN RICE WITH PEAS AND PARMESAN

The ingredients in this homey side dish are just about always in my pantry and fridge. That means I can make it at the drop of a hat. That sure is handy on busy days when I hardly have a second to think about what to prepare for dinner, much less make it to the supermarket to shop for it! **SERVES 4**

1 tablespoon unsalted butter
¼ cup finely chopped onion
2 cups low-sodium chicken broth
2 cups instant brown rice
1 cup frozen peas
1 cup grated Parmesan cheese

1 In a medium saucepan, melt the butter over medium heat. Add the onion and cook, stirring occasionally, until it begins to soften, about 3 minutes.

2 Add the broth, increase the heat to medium-high, and bring to a boil. Stir in the rice and peas and return to a rolling boil. Cover the pan, reduce the heat to low, and cook for 5 minutes. Then stir in the cheese and remove the pan from the heat. Cover the pan and let the rice stand until the broth has been absorbed, about 5 minutes.

BETTER BROTH: I always use low-sodium broths because I like to be in control of the amount of sodium going into my dishes. It's especially important to control the sodium in a recipe like this one that has a cup of salty Parmesan cheese added at the end.

Nutritional count based on 4 servings: 328 calories, 16g protein, 12g fat, 41g carbohydrate, 4g fiber, 551mg sodium

MUSHROOM BROWN RICE

This quick dish is a little tip of the hat to my Mama and my Grandmama's Southern Brown Rice, a delicious, buttery blend of white rice and canned mushrooms that I loved as a kid. In this updated version, I use brown rice, which adds nuttiness to fresh, earthy mushrooms. My easy changes more than halved the calories of the classic I grew up on! The secret is to make sure the dish is really loaded up with mushrooms. I think this straightforward plate of food proves that sometimes it's the simple things in life that are the most pleasing. **SERVES 4**

1 tablespoon olive oil
½ small onion, finely chopped
½ pound baby bella, cremini, or button
    mushrooms, stems trimmed, thinly sliced
¼ teaspoon salt, plus more to taste
Freshly ground black pepper
2 cups hot cooked brown rice

1 In a large skillet, heat the oil over medium heat. Add the onion and cook, stirring occasionally, until it is beginning to soften, about 3 minutes. Add the mushrooms and cook without stirring for 5 minutes, or until wilted and browned. Season with the salt and pepper to taste.

2 Fold the cooked rice into the mushrooms. Adjust the seasonings, and serve.

RIGHT RICE: When it comes to health benefits, brown rice is the clear winner over white rice. White rice is highly refined, and in the process it is stripped of much of the fiber, vitamins, and minerals that are abundant in brown rice. Unfortunately, brown rice takes a notoriously long time to cook—that's why I tend to use microwave rice packets. That way, I can get all the nutritional benefits of whole grains in as little as 90 seconds. Now that's what I call a win-win.

Nutritional count based on 4 servings (does not include salt and black pepper to taste): 153 calories, 4g protein, 5g fat, 25g carbohydrate, 3g fiber, 147mg sodium

WHOLE-GRAIN FRIED RICE

Two clever tricks make this lip-smacking fried rice super fast. The first one is that I use microwave rice cups, in which the rice is precooked and simply needs to be heated in the microwave. In this recipe, I don't even need to microwave the rice because it finishes cooking right in the mix with the rest of the ingredients. The second is that I grate my carrots and onion. It's so much faster than chopping them, and it helps to ensure that you get a taste of veggies in each and every bite. Delicious and efficient. **SERVES 4**

2 tablespoons low-sodium soy sauce

1 teaspoon toasted sesame oil

⅛ teaspoon crushed red pepper flakes,
 or more to taste

1 small red onion

2 small carrots

2 teaspoons olive oil

1¼-inch piece fresh ginger, peeled and finely
 chopped

1 garlic clove, finely chopped

1 egg plus 1 egg white, lightly beaten together

3 cups day-old cooked brown rice,
 or 3 cups microwave whole-grain rice (such
 as Minute brand microwave cups), unheated

2 whole scallions, thinly sliced

¼ cup chopped fresh cilantro, plus more for
 garnish

1 In a small bowl, combine the soy sauce, sesame oil, red pepper flakes, and 1 tablespoon of water.

2 Coarsely grate the onion and carrots into a medium bowl.

3 In a large skillet, heat 1 teaspoon of the olive oil over high heat. When the oil is hot, add the ginger and garlic. Cook for 30 seconds or until fragrant. Add the grated onion and carrot. Cook until the onion softens, about 2 minutes. Add one fourth of the soy sauce mixture and cook, stirring, for 1 minute more. Then scrape the contents of the skillet into a bowl.

4 In the same skillet, heat the remaining 1 teaspoon olive oil over medium-high heat. When the pan is hot and the oil is shimmering, add the egg. Using a wooden spoon, scramble the egg and break it up into pieces, about 30 seconds. Add the rice and scallions, and stir to combine. Press the rice into the bottom of the skillet and let it cook undisturbed for 1 minute, or until the bottom starts to get crispy. Stir the rice and repeat this process again, cooking for 1 to 2 minutes more.

5 Add the remaining soy sauce mixture and the cooked vegetables to the rice, stir to combine, and cook for 1 minute. Remove the skillet from the heat and fold in the cilantro. Transfer the rice to a serving bowl and serve garnished with more cilantro.

Nutritional count based on 4 servings made with regular brown rice (does not include red pepper flakes to taste or cilantro for garnish):
313 calories, 13g protein, 11g fat, 41g carbohydrate, 4g fiber, 387mg sodium

CREAMY SPINACH POLENTA

The milk and mozzarella in this polenta help to make it extra creamy and velvety smooth. But did you know they also up the protein in this indulgent side? Coupled with spinach, which is a nutritional powerhouse in its own right, this luxurious-tasting dish is a surprisingly healthy choice. It serves four as a side dish or two as a hearty meatless main. **SERVES 4**

1¾ cups 2% milk

1 tablespoon unsalted butter

1 teaspoon Paula Deen's House Seasoning (page 49), plus more to taste

¾ cup instant polenta

1 package (10 ounces) frozen spinach, thawed and squeezed of excess liquid

½ cup shredded part-skim mozzarella cheese

In a medium saucepan, combine the milk, butter, House Seasoning, and 1½ cups of water. Bring to a boil over medium-high heat. Slowly whisk in the polenta and cook, stirring constantly with the whisk, until thickened, 2 to 3 minutes. Stir in the spinach and mozzarella, and season with more House Seasoning if you think it needs it.

· ·
Nutritional count based on 4 servings (does not include House Seasoning to taste): 253 calories, 15g protein, 11g fat, 27g carbohydrate, 4g fiber, 713mg sodium

My LOVELY BRIDE, CLAUDIA, has brought so much richness to my life, and I am so grateful for her. One of the more unexpected pleasures she has introduced me to is her love of dessert. It was such a surprising discovery to find out that she had a real, honest-to-goodness sweet tooth. To look at her—petite, trim, and athletic—you'd never guess she loved her desserts. But as it turns out, because she runs in marathons and competes in triathlons, she has the leeway to indulge a little now and again. She has definitely encouraged me to appreciate the sweeter side of life as I never have before.

While Claudia's favorite desserts are carrot cake and key lime pie, throughout the workweek we stick to simpler, more healthful desserts that still feel indulgent. Just because a sweet ending is light, that doesn't mean it can't be luscious. I still use sinful ingredients like chocolate, cream, nuts, and maple syrup. I just use them in moderation and couple them with lighter options like low-fat yogurt, light milk, and lots and lots of fruit.

Because fruity desserts tend to be so easy and quick to pull together, MINTED BERRIES WITH YOGURT CREAM (page 182) is a weekday standby. I can assemble it in under fifteen minutes, less time than it takes to clear the dinner dishes from the table. Throughout the cold winter months, I turn to apples. HOMEY BAKED APPLES (page 189) can be popped in the oven to caramelize and soften while we're eating dinner. They fill the whole house with the aroma of festive spices as they're cooking away.

I've discovered that sweet shakes are also a great way to wrap up a meal. LIGHTER CHOCOLATE-MINT SHAKES (page 183) and FROZEN MANGO SMOOTHIES (page 185) can be blended and poured into to-go cups for a portable dessert. Claudia and I often take them with us when we go for a post-dinner stroll. I can't think of a more relaxing way to cap off a meal.

As I am a good Southern boy, I'd be shirking my duty if I didn't share the beauties of an old-fashioned ambrosia. These layered desserts are classic fare from my Mama's era, but I think this reinvented version fits in well in today's world. I update mine by adding a bit of crunch in the form of low-fat granola. And I skip any creamy additions that generations past were known to add. EASY AMBROSIA (page 193) is a truly modern interpretation of a lovely classic.

The desserts in this chapter fit so well into a busy lifestyle and make everyday eating feel just a little bit more special. In the end, shouldn't that be the goal for just about every meal we sit down to?

BANANA PARFAITS WITH GRANOLA CRUMBLE

Parfaits are the perfect dessert to serve when you've got company over. They are just too pretty not to be shared. And on top of all that, they can be made well in advance and kept in the fridge for you to whip out at the end of the meal.
SERVES 4

1 package (3.4 ounces) instant vanilla pudding
2 cups 1% milk
¾ cup low-fat granola
2 large bananas, thinly sliced
1 cup fat-free frozen whipped topping, thawed

1 In a medium bowl, whisk together the instant pudding and the milk until combined. Transfer to the refrigerator and chill until cold and set, about 5 minutes.

2 Place 1 tablespoon of the granola in each of four parfait glasses. Top with half of the pudding, half of the banana slices, and half of the whipped topping. Repeat the layering with another tablespoon of granola, the remaining pudding, the remaining bananas, and the remaining whipped topping. Sprinkle the top of each parfait with the remaining tablespoon of granola.

BROWN BANANA: Because I generally make these parfaits in advance, I usually give my bananas a little spritz of lemon, lime, or pineapple juice to keep them from browning (or oxidizing) around the edges. The acid in citrus stops the bananas from oxidizing as they come in contact with the air.

Nutritional count based on 4 servings: 318 calories, 7g protein, 5g fat, 64g carbohydrate, 3g fiber, 465mg sodium

MINTED BERRIES WITH YOGURT CREAM

Clean, fresh flavors: That's what this dessert is all about. To my taste, it's exactly what a dessert should be, especially a midweek one. This is the kind of sweet bite that puts a nice finish on a fine meal but doesn't weigh you down in the evening hours. **SERVES 4**

4 cups mixed berries, such as blueberries, raspberries, and sliced strawberries
⅓ cup chopped fresh mint, plus 4 mint sprigs for garnish
1 cup low-fat plain yogurt
1 tablespoon honey
1 teaspoon vanilla extract

1 In a large bowl, combine the berries and the chopped mint. Let them stand for 10 minutes at room temperature.

2 Meanwhile, in a small bowl, whisk together the yogurt, honey, and vanilla until smooth.

3 Divide the berries among four bowls. Drizzle the yogurt cream over the top, and garnish with the mint sprigs.

Nutritional count based on 4 servings: 135 calories, 5g protein, 2g fat, 27g carbohydrate, 6g fiber, 47mg sodium

LIGHTER CHOCOLATE-MINT SHAKES

You know those after-dinner mints that some fancy restaurants give you at the end of your meal? Well, imagine those tasty little morsels as a frosty, creamy treat and you pretty much have the idea of this sweet ending. While it tastes sinfully bad for you, it's actually a light take on the classic malted shake. **SERVES 4**

1 pint chocolate sorbet

1 cup 1% milk

⅛ teaspoon peppermint extract

8 tablespoons prepared whipped light cream

1 hard peppermint candy, crushed

In a blender, combine the sorbet, milk, and peppermint extract and blend until smooth. Divide among four 8-ounce glasses, and garnish with the whipped cream and crushed peppermint candy.

Nutritional count based on 4 servings: 101 calories, 2g protein, 1g fat, 21g carbohydrate, 0g fiber, 43mg sodium

FROZEN MANGO SMOOTHIES

Here's a dessert that comes together in the push of a button. Just toss all the ingredients into a blender and blend until smooth. When you need to satisfy a sweet tooth craving, it sure doesn't get much easier than this. **SERVES 2**

2 cups fresh or frozen mango chunks

1⅓ cups 1% milk

1 cup small ice cubes

¼ cup fat-free Greek yogurt

2 tablespoons honey

1 teaspoon vanilla extract

Combine all the ingredients in a blender and blend until frothy and smooth. Divide the smoothie between two 8-ounce glasses, and serve.

FROZEN ASSETS: I keep my freezer stocked with all types of frozen fruits. That way I can make smoothies using any fruit I've got on hand, even when that fruit is out of season. Needless to say, this smoothie is delicious with whatever fruit you've got in your freezer.

Nutritional count based on 2 servings: 262 calories, 8g protein, 2g fat, 56g carbohydrate, 3g fiber, 99mg sodium

STRAWBERRY ANGEL FOOD CAKE

One teaspoon of sugar may look a little skimpy, but given that angel food cakes tend to be plenty sweet on their own, you really don't need to add much sugar to this dessert. And of course, there's the natural sweetness of the raspberries and strawberries. Who knew strawberries in a raspberry sauce would taste so good? This pretty little confection will be a happy surprise. **SERVES 8**

¾ cup frozen raspberries, thawed
1 teaspoon superfine sugar
1 pound strawberries, hulled and quartered
1 store-bought angel food cake (7-inch diameter)

1 Working over a medium bowl, use a rubber spatula or the back of a large spoon to press the raspberries through a fine-mesh strainer. You should end up with ¼ cup of juice. Stir the sugar into the juice until dissolved. Add the strawberries and toss until evenly coated.

2 Serve the cake topped with the raspberry syrup–covered strawberries.

KEEP MOVING: While I realize it's awfully tempting to pack it in for the day and head straight for the couch after dinner, I highly recommend you don't succumb to that temptation. Try a walk around the block or a few throws of the football in the backyard with your kid after you've finished your evening meal, especially if dessert figured into it. A little bit of exercise will do a world of good after the big meal and will actually help you sleep more soundly.

Nutritional count based on 8 servings: 52 calories, 1g protein, 0g fat, 13g carbohydrate, 2g fiber, 27mg sodium

HOMEY BAKED APPLES

Sometimes the simplest desserts are the best. Pop these in the oven as you are sitting down for dinner and you will have a homemade dessert ready and waiting for you when you finish up your entrées. These are also a great addition to any Thanksgiving dessert table, for those looking for something a little less decadent than pumpkin pie but still as satisfying. **SERVES 4**

4 baking apples (5 to 6 ounces each),
    such as McIntosh
4 teaspoons unsalted butter
⅛ teaspoon ground cinnamon
4 teaspoons pure maple syrup
Vanilla frozen yogurt, for serving (optional)

1 Preheat the oven to 400°F. Grease an 8-inch square baking dish with cooking spray.

2 Core the apples, making sure not to cut through the bottom, creating a 2-teaspoon cavity. Peel away 1 inch of the skin from around the top of the cavity. Press 1 teaspoon of the butter into the bottom of each cavity. Sprinkle the cinnamon over the butter, and top with the maple syrup. Place the apples in the prepared baking dish, and pour in enough water to cover the bottom of the dish by ¼ inch. Bake until tender, about 25 minutes.

3 Serve in bowls, with a scoop of frozen yogurt (if using) and the pan juices drizzled on top.

Nutritional count based on 4 servings (does not include vanilla frozen yogurt for serving): 128 calories, 1g protein, 4g fat, 25g carbohydrate, 4g fiber, 2mg sodium

PEACH ICE CREAM SUNDAES

Even though I come from the fresh peach state, I have always had a weakness for canned peaches. When I was a kid, I used to eat them straight out of the tin. This grown-up treatment of canned peaches is more my speed these days. Cinnamon, cloves, and almond extract add a touch of the exotic to this comfort food of my youth. The creamy vanilla yogurt and crunchy almonds round out this decadent-tasting but decidedly healthy dessert. **SERVES 4**

1 can (15 ounces) light peaches,
 coarsely chopped
½ teaspoon ground cinnamon
Pinch of ground cloves
½ teaspoon almond extract
1½ cups vanilla frozen yogurt
½ cup coarsely chopped blanched almonds

1 In a large skillet, stir together the peaches, ¼ teaspoon of the cinnamon, and the cloves. Cook, stirring, over medium-high heat until the liquid is reduced and thickened, 15 to 20 minutes. Stir in the almond extract. Remove from the heat and let cool slightly, 5 to 10 minutes.

2 Scoop the frozen yogurt into individual bowls and top with the peaches. Sprinkle with the chopped almonds and the remaining ¼ teaspoon cinnamon, and serve immediately.

Nutritional count based on 4 servings: 210 calories, 5g protein, 8g fat, 32g carbohydrate, 3g fiber, 47mg sodium

RASPBERRY MOUSSE

Don't limit yourself to raspberries when you're in the mood for this light and fluffy mousse. If it's frozen blueberries you've got on hand, go ahead and make it blueberry mousse. Same goes for any other frozen berry or fruit you've got in your freezer. Just be sure to cook the fruit down to a thick, syrupy consistency and to give it a good stir through the whipped topping so that you get great fruity flavor in every bite. **SERVES 4**

2 cups (10 ounces) frozen raspberries
Grated zest and juice of 1 lime
½ teaspoon vanilla extract
1 ounce (2 tablespoons) white tequila (optional)
3 cups light frozen whipped topping, thawed

1 In a medium saucepan, stir together the raspberries, lime zest, and lime juice. Cook over medium heat, using the back of a wooden spoon to crush the berries, until they are warmed through and the sauce has thickened, about 12 minutes. Stir in the vanilla and tequila (if using), and place in the freezer to cool completely, about 10 minutes.

2 Spoon the whipped topping into a medium bowl and, using a rubber spatula, gently fold in the chilled berry puree. Serve the mousse immediately.

WHIP IT UP: Light whipped topping is something you'll always find in my freezer. Having it on hand means I've always got the beginnings of a delicious, airy dessert that won't break the calorie bank.

Nutritional count based on 4 servings (does not include optional tequila): 257 calories, 3g protein, 8g fat, 46g carbohydrate, 6g fiber, 42mg sodium

EASY AMBROSIA

Good old-fashioned ambrosia is the very definition of sweet Southern beauty. Traditionally it's served alongside the savory main dish, but I prefer to bring it out for dessert. I use sweetened coconut in this version, so there's no need to add in extra sugar. And I lighten up the dish by skipping the classic heavy cream and marshmallows my Mama used to stir through hers. My ambrosia is a pretty little dish that takes just minutes to assemble. **SERVES 4**

4 large navel oranges (about 2 pounds)
4 pitted dried dates (about 2 ounces), thinly sliced
2 tablespoons shredded sweetened coconut
2 tablespoons low-fat granola

1 Working with one orange at a time and using a sharp knife, cut a thin slice off the top and bottom of the orange so you can see the orange flesh. Working your knife along the curve of the orange, trim off all the peel and the white pith, leaving the orange flesh. Slice the peeled orange crosswise into ¼-inch-thick rounds and lay them out on a serving plate.

2 Scatter the dates and coconut over the oranges. Sprinkle with the granola, and serve.

Nutritional count based on 4 servings: 58 calories, 1g protein, 2g fat, 11g carbohydrate, 1g fiber, 10mg sodium

PANTRY IDEAS

🛒 STOCKING UP

One of the best ways to ensure that you don't turn to fast food throughout the busy week is to make sure you've got the ingredients on hand for delicious, healthy homemade meals. Stock up your fridge and pantry over the weekend with foods that get you prepared for the work-week. Having the right ingredients in your kitchen saves you time and money so that you can whip up quick, easy, good-for-you meals at the drop of a hat. Here's a starter list of basic supplies that I've found handy to have around.

In the Pantry

- Baking supplies (flour, sugars, cornstarch, baking powder and soda, vanilla extract)
- Beans (canned: kidney, black, chickpea, cannellini)
- Breads and wraps (whole-wheat and whole-grain)
- Broths and soups
- Fish (canned tuna and salmon)
- Fruit (canned and fresh: apples, bananas, pears, pineapple, peaches)
- Grains (barley, bulgur, couscous, grits, brown rice)
- Herbs and spices (dried: coriander, crushed red pepper flakes, cumin, garlic powder, oregano, Paula Deen's House Seasoning)
- Honey
- Oats and nuts
- Oils and cooking spray
- Onions and garlic
- Pastas
- Tomatoes (canned: crushed, diced, paste, sauce, whole)
- Vinegars

In the Fridge

- Butter
- Cheeses (Cheddar, feta, Parmesan, cream cheese [Neufchâtel])
- Condiments (ketchup, mustards, light mayo)
- Eggs
- Fruits (berries, grapes, citrus, peaches, plums, grapes)
- Herbs (fresh basil, cilantro, parsley, thyme)
- Hot sauces
- Meat (bacon [turkey and pork], beef, chicken, deli meats, lamb, pork, turkey)
- Milk (skim and 1%)
- Seafood
- Vegetables (bell peppers, broccoli, carrots, cucumbers, green beans, mushrooms, lettuces, tomatoes, zucchini, kale)
- Yogurt

In the Freezer

- Berries and other fruits
- Corn kernels
- Meats
- Mixed vegetables
- Peas
- Shrimp
- Spinach
- Waffles, whole-wheat
- Whipped topping (fat-free and light)

 ## INSTANT WEEKNIGHT PANTRY MEALS

We all need a helping hand with dinner now and again. Here are some ideas for meals made with healthy prepared products. These shortcuts will help you get dinner together even faster than you can say "takeout."

Frozen Mixed Vegetable Stir-Fry

A bag of frozen mixed vegetables can provide you with a full day's supply of vitamins. And it tastes a lot better! I warm the mixed vegetables in a wok with a little toasted sesame oil, then add flavor by stirring in bottled teriyaki sauce. I serve this stir-fry over instant brown rice to create a complete meal in minutes.

Rotisserie Chicken Quesadillas

I absolutely love supermarket rotisserie chicken. I often have one on hand in the fridge for quick lunches and dinners. However, I always take the skin off and discard it. While it is delicious, it's packed with fat that I don't need in my diet. One of my favorite uses for rotisserie chicken is as a stuffing for quesadillas. I top a whole-wheat tortilla with chicken, thawed frozen corn, and shredded Cheddar and warm it up in the oven until the tortilla is crisp and the cheese is melted. I top the quesadilla with bagged lettuce leaves, give it a squirt of lime juice, and dinner is served.

Sausages on Chickpea Couscous

It never ceases to amaze me that couscous takes a mere five minutes to prepare. For this quick dish, I stir rinsed and drained chickpeas through hot cooked whole-wheat couscous. To top the bean-couscous mixture, I slice up precooked flavored chicken sausage and give it a quick pan-fry. Then I douse the whole delicious mixture with a spicy tomato-based sauce that I'm absolutely loving right now. It's called Sriracha and you can find it in the international section of most supermarkets. If your local market doesn't have Sriracha, your favorite hot sauce will do just fine.

Black Bean Nachos

While I stay away from this dish in most restaurants, at home I make my own healthy version that satisfies my cravings for nachos. I use whole-grain baked tortilla chips as my base and top them with shredded Cheddar, rinsed and drained black beans, and jarred sliced jalapeños. I warm the platter up in the oven until the cheese has melted all over, then serve it with diced fresh avocado, some fresh salsa, and plenty of lime wedges.

Tuna and Spinach Salad

I'm crazy for spinach salads. You could top them with just about anything and I'd be a fan, but top one with canned tuna and you have me as a friend for life. For this protein-packed dinner, I toss spinach leaves with jarred black olives, halved cherry tomatoes, sliced cucumbers, and a light citrusy bottled dressing. Then I add the flaked, drained tuna and give it a good grind of black pepper before digging right in.

Baked Artichoke Frittata

Jarred marinated artichoke hearts add instant flavor to a quick-cooking frittata without any work. The trick is to give them a good rinse before chopping them up. This gets rid of some of the excess oil. Then just beat up some eggs, stir in the artichokes, with maybe a pinch of crushed red pepper flakes and some Parmesan cheese, and bake the frittata at 300°F until it just sets. Easy and tasty and you can eat the leftovers in a sandwich the next day.

Sun-Dried Tomato Pizza

I love to keep balls of whole-wheat pizza dough in the freezer so I can whip up a healthy meal that's good enough for company—I mean, who doesn't love pizza? Just let the dough defrost on the counter for about an hour or two (or take it out and stick it in the fridge before you leave for work), then roll it out and top it with slivers of sun-dried tomatoes, your favorite tomato sauce, some shredded mozzarella, and some dried oregano. Bake at 400°F until it's bubbling and brown. Pizza delivery has nothing on this!

Instant White Bean and Winter Squash Soup

Canned beans are not only some of the most nutritious pantry items to keep on hand, they are also easy to turn into an instant meal. Throw a couple of cans of rinsed white beans into a pot with some chicken or vegetable stock and a box of frozen pureed winter squash, then let it simmer for about 10 minutes. Puree it if you like it smooth, and serve it with some fresh lemon juice and chopped parsley. It's warming, filling, and so good for you.

Easy Shrimp Burgers

Because they freeze them when they're super fresh, frozen shrimp are just about as good as fresh, and I love knowing there's a bag of them on hand for last-minute suppers. You can throw them in pasta or sauté them with garlic. Or to make a tasty shrimp burger, chop up the shrimp and season well with mustard, hot sauce, garlic, and scallions or onions. Add a scoop or two of breadcrumbs, then form patties and broil until crisp. I like to serve them open-faced on whole-wheat buns with plenty of lettuce and tomatoes—and a few dashes of hot sauce.

Sesame-Baked Tofu

Did you know that you can keep a box of tofu in your fridge for over a month (make sure to check the sell-by date, though, so you know it's fresh when you get it)? This makes getting a healthy dinner on the table a snap—even when you think there's nothing in the house to eat. I like to buy extra-firm tofu since it's the meatiest. Just blot it dry, and cover it with a marinade made from low-sodium soy sauce, a little sesame oil, red pepper flakes, a squirt of honey, and a touch of lemon juice or rice wine vinegar. Then bake in a hot oven until it's golden brown all over. Serve it over baby lettuce or spinach if you've got some. It also makes a mean sandwich.

DINING OUT SMART

Just because you've committed to eating healthy doesn't mean you have to give up on eating out. Armed with these clever tips and tricks, you can feel good about restaurant dining any old day of the week.

Share your meal with a friend

I have discovered that restaurant portions are almost always more than I can or should be eating in one sitting. Most of the time, I like to have my own starter and then split my main with my dining partner. On our first date out, I found out that Claudia liked to dine this way too. I realized right then and there that I'd found a soul mate.

Skip the bread

I don't even let my server place the basket of bread on my table. If it's there, you can bet I'll start nibbling. If it's not in sight, I find I don't miss it at all.

Limit your alcohol

Dining out can be an excuse for one too many glasses of wine or beer. That means extra empty calories. If I do feel like a drink, I stick to just one with my main course.

Look for light menu options

Many restaurant menus now feature a section called "Lighter Fare" or something along those lines. I have discovered that these meals are often better than the regular menu dishes. They tend to be made to order, so they come out super fresh.

Bring your own dressing

You might feel a bit silly the first time you do it, but you'll quickly see results from bringing your own homemade low-fat dressings to restaurants. Salads can be a fat and calorie trap in many dining establishments. Asking them to hold the dressing and using your own is just smart eating. If you don't want to bring your own, be sure to ask for the restaurant's dressing on the side, and add it sparingly to your salad.

Read the nutritional information

Large chain restaurants are now required to post nutritional information for their dishes. Being informed about what you are eating is integral to eating right. Pay attention to these stats. You'll find some surprises, like a hearty steak dish with fewer calories than what you may have figured was a low-calorie plate of fish.

Split the Dessert (or, one dessert, four forks)

When it comes to a sweet finish to a meal, my rule is simple: one dessert, four forks. I never order dessert unless I've got three other people to share it with. If a full serving is put in front of me, the temptation to clear the plate can be too strong when all I really need after a satisfying restaurant meal is a sweet little bite to cap the evening off.

Never Drink Your Calories

Unless we're talking about a glass of wine or a light beer, I try not to drink any calories when I'm dining out. That means no sweet iced tea, no sodas (except for club soda or diet soda), and no juice. That leaves me plenty of room to enjoy my meal and maybe even a bite of dessert.

A WEEK OF MENUS UNDER 1,500 CALORIES PER DAY

Pull it all together for a week of healthy menus that come in under 1,500 calories per day: breakfast, lunch, dinner, and dessert and/or snack. (All calorie counts are approximate.)

SUNDAY (1,486 CALORIES)

While I try to eat healthy each and every day, on Sunday I loosen things up a bit. Not every meal clocks in at less than 350 calories. And that's okay! I may eat a little more on my day of rest, but I make sure what I'm putting into my body is as healthy as what I'm eating throughout the workweek.

- **BREAKFAST (433):** Tomato Grits and Sausage (170) topped with a large fried egg (93) and served with a slice of whole-wheat toast (70) spread with 1 tablespoon unsalted butter (100)
- **LUNCH (504):** Oven-Fried Chicken Po'Boys (337; page 70) with a side of Roasted Parsnips (167; page 151)
- **SNACK (90):** Small banana
- **DINNER (401):** Roasted Pork Tenderloin with Onions and Carrots (216; page 95) served with a baked sweet potato (162) topped with 1 tablespoon of low-fat Greek yogurt (23)
- **DESSERT: (58)** Easy Ambrosia (page 193)

MONDAY (1,324 CALORIES)

My name for this day is Meatless Monday. After a busy weekend, I choose to start the workweek off with a meat-free, vegetable-packed menu. This lineup keeps things lean and green.

- **BREAKFAST (331):** ½ grapefruit (41) and 1 whole-wheat English muffin (130) spread with 1 tablespoon unsalted butter (100) and topped with slices of ¼ medium Hass avocado (60)
- **LUNCH (315):** Quick Vegetable Minestrone (165; page 27) with ½ serving Niçoise Salad (150; page 14)
- **SNACK (332):** 2 ounces dry-roasted salted peanuts

DINNER (346): Sunny-Side-Up Portobello Burger (263; page 121) with Lemony Cabbage Slaw (61; page 158) and ½ cup steamed green beans (22)

TUESDAY (1,303 CALORIES)

By Tuesday morning, the workweek is in full swing. I need to be up and out the door quickly. A mango smoothie is a healthy portable breakfast that helps me get going fast. While I often skip dessert on Mondays, on Tuesdays I slot a healthy sweet treat back into the menu.

BREAKFAST (262): Frozen Mango Smoothie (page 185)

LUNCH (245): Three-Bean and Kale Chili (211; page 116) and 1 cup cherry tomato salad (27) with 1 tablespoon fat-free dressing (7)

SNACK (245): 1 container (6 ounces) low-fat blueberry yogurt (170) and 1 small apple (75)

DINNER (341): One-Pan Roasted Chicken and Broccoli (270; page 73) with Sweet and Spicy Baked Sweet Potatoes (71; page 160)

DESSERT (210): Peach Ice Cream Sundae (page 190)

WEDNESDAY: (1,270 CALORIES)

I like to treat myself to my favorite dishes on Wednesday nights, a reward for making it halfway to the weekend! A plate of scallops and grits is high on that list, and angel food cake completes the meal perfectly.

BREAKFAST (217): Italian Vegetable Frittata (134; page 106) and 1 cup blueberries (83)

LUNCH (349): Whole-Wheat Italian Pasta Salad (245; page 171) with a green salad of 2 cups lettuce and 1 tablespoon fat-free dressing (23) and a small pear (81)

SNACK (312): 2 slices low-fat Swiss cheese (140) with 10 whole-wheat crackers (120) and ½ cup seedless green grapes (52)

DINNER (340): Light and Easy Scallops and Grits (225; page 45) with Roasted Brussels Sprouts (115; page 147)

DESSERT (52): Strawberry Angel Food Cake (page 186)

THURSDAY (1,298 CALORIES)

When I have the time to pop back home for lunch, quesadillas are a delicious and quick midday meal. The fixings for my famous Mushroom Spinach Quesadillas are almost always on hand in my kitchen.

BREAKFAST (222): Baked Eggs with Tomatoes, Onions, and Peppers (page 108)

LUNCH (342): Mushroom Spinach Quesadillas (269; page 111) and 1 large peach (73)

SNACK (283): 1 bar (1½ ounces) dark chocolate (218) and 1 small orange (65)

DINNER (323): Bourbon-Braised Pork Chops (238; page 99) with Big Ol' Pot of Greens (85; page 153)

DESSERT (128): Homey Baked Apples (page 189)

FRIDAY (1,358 CALORIES)

You'll find me firing up the grill on Fridays. It gets me in a festive mood for the weekend ahead. For lunch I keep it light and healthy with California Turkey Burgers. At dinner I invite some friends around for a juicy steak, open a bottle of red wine, and raise a glass to a week well spent.

BREAKFAST (276): 2 whole-wheat frozen waffles (170) with 1 tablespoon pure maple syrup (53) and 1 cup sliced strawberries (53)

LUNCH (315): California Turkey Burgers (307; page 132) and ½ cup air-popped popcorn (8)

SNACK (100): 1 chocolate chip granola bar

DINNER (349): Chimichurri Steaks (195; page 135) with Quinoa, Black Bean, and Corn Salad (154; page 172)

DESSERT (318): Banana Parfaits with Granola Crumble (page 180)

SATURDAY (1,379 CALORIES)

Saturday is my favorite day of the week. I wake up early and eat a quick breakfast so that I can get on with the day. Claudia and I like to head out for a run in the morning and then hit the farmers' market for fresh produce for the week. After a busy morning, the rest of Saturday is for relaxing and catching up with friends and family.

BREAKFAST (172): 1 cup bran cereal (120) with ½ cup skim milk (20) and ½ cup sliced strawberries (32)

LATE MORNING SNACK (101): Lighter Chocolate-Mint Shakes (page 183)

LUNCH (332): Grilled Cumin Chicken and Potato Salad (315; page 130) with 1 cup baby spinach leaves dressed with 1 tablespoon balsamic vinegar (17)

AFTERNOON SNACK (290): 10 baked pita chips (150) with ¼ cup hummus (140)

DINNER (349): Ham-Stuffed Trout (317; page 128) with 5 grilled asparagus spears (32)

DESSERT (135): Minted Berries with Yogurt Cream (page 182)

ACKNOWLEDGMENTS

As always, I'm sending out a big thank-you and warm hug to each and every member of my family. A special shout out is in order to Mama, Michael, and Jamie for putting their minds to getting healthy these past couple years. You are all such an inspiration to me. The recipes in this book are a perfect fit for your new and improved lifestyle. And, of course, I wouldn't be the person I am without the love and support of my father, Jimmy Deen, who is an incredibly special person in my life. Thanks also to my fantastic friends, including, of course, Sam Carter. I can always count on you to push me to be my very best every day.

Big thanks to my editor, Pamela Cannon, and the entire Ballantine Books team, including Liz Cosgrove, Joe Perez, Mark Maguire, Nancy Delia, Betsy Wilson, and Alison Masciovecchio. I think y'all are the best in the business.

Thanks to photographer Ben Fink for making my food look as good as it tastes. And thanks to María del Mar Sacasa for all of her thoughtful preparation and styling during the shoot.

Thank you also to my writing and recipe-editing team: Nancy Duran, Sarah Huck, Karen Rush, Julia Heffelfinger, Rebekah Peppler, Adelaide Mueller, and Jeanne McLaurin. You make my vision come to life.

To the gang at The Lady & Sons Restaurant, I love and appreciate y'all so much. My utter trust in you gives me the ability to get projects like this done. Heartfelt thanks also to the whole crew at Paula Deen Enterprises, most especially Sarah Meighen.

Happy cooking everybody. And here's to making every day count!

INDEX

(Page references in *italic* refer to illustrations.)